CHILDREN'S ENCYCLOPEDIA

SPACE AND UNIVERSE

Contents

Universe	5
Earth	14
Planets and Satellites	35
The Sun	61
The Moon	87
Stars	113
Galaxies	131
The History of Astronomy	142

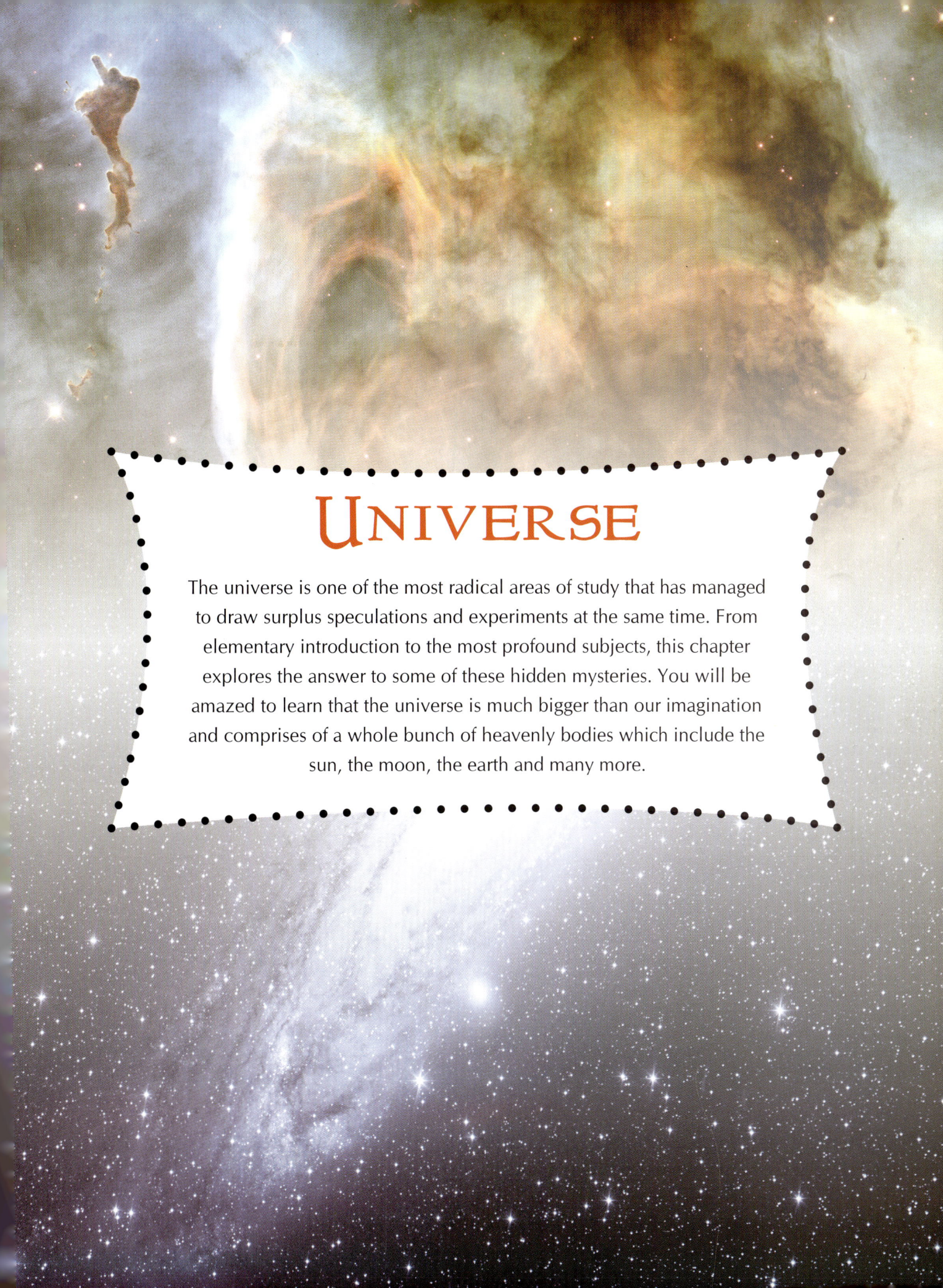

Universe

The universe is one of the most radical areas of study that has managed to draw surplus speculations and experiments at the same time. From elementary introduction to the most profound subjects, this chapter explores the answer to some of these hidden mysteries. You will be amazed to learn that the universe is much bigger than our imagination and comprises of a whole bunch of heavenly bodies which include the sun, the moon, the earth and many more.

The fascinating universe

Have you ever taken time out from your engagements and gave a thought on the world around us? When it all started? How it all happened? The word UNIVERSE is understood as the perfect piece of a tempting pie with correct amount of sugar, flavour and all the goodies that will give you a wholesome experience. But that's not all, when we talk about the universe, many ingredients comes into play (the sun, the satellites, stars and many more). You will be amazed to learn that we are not alone, as countless planets, solar systems, stars and galaxies accompany our relatively tiny planet, called Earth.

When we look up at the night sky, most of the celestial objects we see with the naked eye are stars that are within the Milky Way. But two of these objects are so distant that we know the Universe does not end with the Milky Way. These are the Magellanic Clouds, which can be seen from Earth in the southern hemisphere, and the Andromeda galaxy, which can be seen from the northern hemisphere-with a little more difficulty.

More than One Universe?

It is difficult to answer questions about the Universe, because some scientists think the Universe is everything that exists. Others think of our Universe as just part of something even larger. They believe there may be other universes separate from ours which we cannot see.

The beginning of time Scientific research shows that the known Universe started at a certain point in time and may some day end. What was there before? What will there be after? We cannot look at the Universe form the outside. We cannot imagine an end to time, or a limit to space. It is for these reasons that some scientists believe there must be something outside our Universe.

If the stars of the Universe were spread out evenly in every direction across the sky, with no dark matter in between light would come from every point in the sky. At this point the sky would be as bright as the surface of the Sun.

The night sky appears dark, not completely bright as it would be if light had come from stars in every direction. The only reason for this can be that the Universe does have a limit- in space and time.

The Universe is made up of all the galaxies grouped together in large clusters [1]. Each galaxy, like our Milky Way [2], is made up of thousands of millions of stars, one of which is our Sun, accompanied by its planets [3].

Swift Move

The magnitude of the speed of light or radio waves in a vacuum is approximately 186,000 miles per second. This is the fastest radiant energy- a radio and light waves can cover. They outshine the spaceships in the race. If a spaceship orbited at 99.94% of the speed of light, 68 years would pass on the spaceship while 2,000 years passed on Earth.

Calculating Distances

To measure the distances between the planetary bodies is a tricky task. They can be determined by bouncing a radar signal off their surface. The time it takes for the signal to return tells us how far the object is. In June, it has been observed that a very distant star is always seen in a slightly altered position than it is in December, when the sun is extreme opposite to the earth.

Know your Home

Try to look at a sparkling sky at night. You will notice the silvery band of stars- we call it the Milky Way. Our Earth, the Moon, and the other planets along with its satellites comprise the Milky Way. It has been a subject of spectacle for many. From ancient civilisations, these heavenly bodies have been embodied as deities and Supreme Beings. The Milky Way is made up of countless individual stars. Dark areas in the Milky Way aren't empty spaces. Here, huge clouds of dust absorb the light from the stars and beyond. The Milky Way is a kind of rotating disk with a huge concentration at the centre and curved spiralling arms. It consists of a whooping 200 billion stars, along with number of gaseous substances and dust.

Dark Matter

The practical definition to this theory is waiting for an explicit answer. But scholars/experts in the realm of science presume that there is much more matter in the Milky Way than what is observed. In addition to visible stars and dust, there must be colossal quantity of dark matter in the space. Scientist believe that dark matter consist almost entirely of unknown nuclear particles.

Light Year

A Light Year is the distance in which the light travels in a vacuum in one Julian year. A numerical term, mostly used by non-specialist and space enthusiast, a light-year is a unit to measure distances to stars and other stellar bodies.

Age Factor

The average age limit of a human being is 80-100 years. But you will be surprised to know that our Universe is there since time infinite. With little effort on your part even you can spot the inherent changes taking places all around. Profound observations from experts show us that there is change in the universe. The stars and planets are created and also can perish. Application of advanced methods has enabled us to determine the age of the rocks, even if they are more than 100 billion years old. We have not found a single rock in our Earth that is more than 4 billion years old. There is also a reason to consider that the solar system has a limited age: the sun only has enough fuel for about 11 billion years. With indications that it has been shinning for about 5 billion years, the sun still has 6 billion years to go.

The Beginning

Today, we find that the galaxies are moving away from each other. This suggest that they might have been closer once and extremely compact. If Laws of Physics are accurate, then we conclude that this heavenly body has been extremely hot. Since planets, stars, galaxies and even atoms cannot exist at extremely high temperature; the young universe might have been nothing more than a mixture of hot, densely packed elementary particles with high energy radiation. After the big bang, the newly born universe changed very rapidly. Scientists are yet to uncover the mystery of the first 10(-43) seconds of the explosion- that's 0.0000000000000000000000000000000000000 0001 seconds.

Fundamental Forces

In general knowledge, there are four fundamental forces in nature. The gravity that causes an apple to fall to the ground and holds the Moon in its orbit around the earth is one. Another one is the electromagnetic force we see when magnetic poles attract or repel. The other two forces are the weak and strong nuclear forces. The strong nuclear force is particularly essential. It holds together, protons and neutrons and keeps them in the nucleus of the atom. On the other hand, the strong nuclear force and the electromagnetic force only affect certain particles; gravity and the weak nuclear force affect all elementary particles.

GUT

Gut stands for Grand Unified Theory. This theory describes how the different fundamental forces are related to each other.

The Miller Theory

A chemistry student, by the name Stanley Miller in 1953 conducted an experiment. He filled a glass of container with water and added some mixture of gases that had existed in the Earth's early atmosphere. Then he ran an electrical current through this controlled "environment"- imitating a bolt of lightening. This resulted in the formation of organic molecules- the basic elements of life.

Predictions

According to reports, the universe will continue expanding. In about 6 billion years, the sun will die out having used all its fuel. And at some point, however, there will be no more matter from which to form new stars. Predictions are been made that one day all the matter in the universe will have decayed. After about 1000 years there won't be any galaxies either- they will have lost more and more star remnants into the space. Other parts of the galaxies will be drawn into the huge, central black holes and only a few white dwarves, neutron stars, smaller black holes, and some gases, dust, and radiation will remain.

Thousands of Millions of Stars

Both these objects are galaxies outside the Milky Way. If, as astronomers think, the average galaxy is made up of thousands of millions of stars, and the Universe contains thousands of millions of galaxies, how big is the Universe?

God Factor

From time immemorial, people carry the divine belief in God's creation of the Universe. It still holds true in the heart of many believers. No science has been able to completely dismiss or accept the theory of the existence of a Supreme Being. When scientists study atoms and galaxies, it still doesn't tell us whether they were created by a higher being or not. It is entirely possible to study quarks, black holes and solar eclipses and still believe in God.

The Laws of the Universe

The Moon revolves around the Earth, which revolves around the Sun. The law of gravity is responsible for this phenomenon and for the fact that the stars of the galaxies stay together and that comets travel through the entire universe along a trajectory that we can calculate. All heavenly bodies move in space according to the laws of celestial mechanics.

Kepler's Laws

The ancients considered that the Earth was the centre of the universe and that all the heavenly bodies revolved around it. **Copernicus**, in the sixteenth century, revolutionised astronomy when he declared that the Sun was the centre and that the remaining planets, including the Earth, moved around it, although he could not explain how they did so. In the seventeenth century, it was **Kepler** who figured out how that movement worked. After many observations and calculations, he declared that the planets revolve around the Sun along elliptical orbits. He also explained how that works in three laws that bear his name.

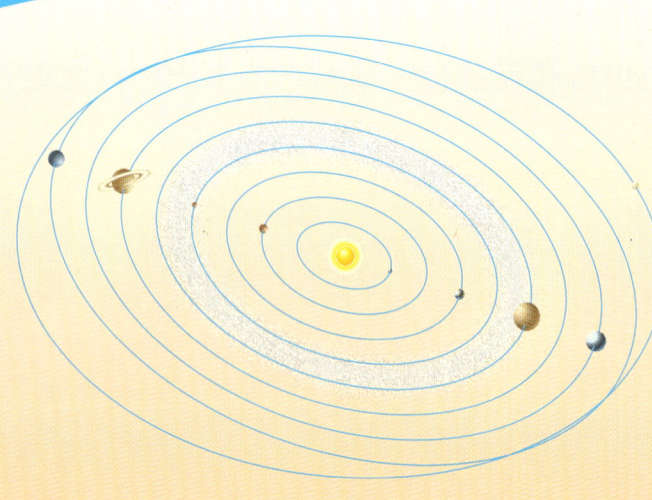

In the solar system, the planets trace an ellipse around the Sun.

First Law
Each planet moves in an elliptical orbit and the Sun is one of the foci of the ellipse.

Second Law
The closer the planets are to the Sun in their trajectory, the faster they move.

Third Law
The further a planet is from the Sun, the greater its speed of revolution.

EXPANSION OF THE UNIVERSE

One proof of the expansion of the universe is the fact that the galaxies that comprise it are moving away from one another. Observations from the Earth, which is part of a galaxy, show that the other galaxies are moving further away from us, and the more distant they are, the faster they are moving. The galaxies at the outer reaches of the universe are the ones that were born first—in other words, the oldest ones—and they are moving at a speed that approaches that of light, which is the greatest speed possible.

The most distant galaxies are moving at a speed of around 165,000 miles (270,000 kilometres) per second.

Earth

Home to the human beings, this blue planet is the most important celestial body in existence. The Earth is the mother of mankind and this chapter is a detailed illustration of the world we live in. Know and understand your surroundings in a better way and have an immaculate picture of the myriad facts that make up the story of the planet Earth.

Our very own Earth

Our lovely Earth is the only planet that support's life. Earth is the supreme owner of the most important source of existence: water, which covers almost 3/4th of its surface area.

What a relief!!
Most importantly, to our relief, Earth's atmosphere is full of oxygen for us to breath. It will never run out of service.

Our planet Earth, together with other planets, satellites and smaller bodies, forms part of the Solar System. The Sun, the central star of our Solar System, is one of the thousands of millions of stars that make up our galaxy, the Milky Way. This galaxy is just one of the countless galaxies that fill our universe.

Three major differences
The Earth differs from the rest of the planets in three important ways. First, it has water in liquid form which covers most of its surface. The planet Mars and some satellites have water in the form of ice on their surfaces, but at present, no other body has liquid water.

Second, Earth's **atmosphere** is mostly **oxygen.** The atmospheres of Venus and Mars are mainly **carbon dioxide** and those of the largest or giant planets (Jupiter, Saturn, Uranus and Neptune) are mostly hydrogen.

Third, and most important, there is life on Earth. Up to now, no form of life has been found anywhere else in the Solar System. Primitive forms of life may exist on a satellite of one of the giant planets but none has yet been found.

Planet Earth is one of the terrestrial planets along with Mercury, Venus and Mars. Further from the Sun are the four giant planets and then tiny Pluto.

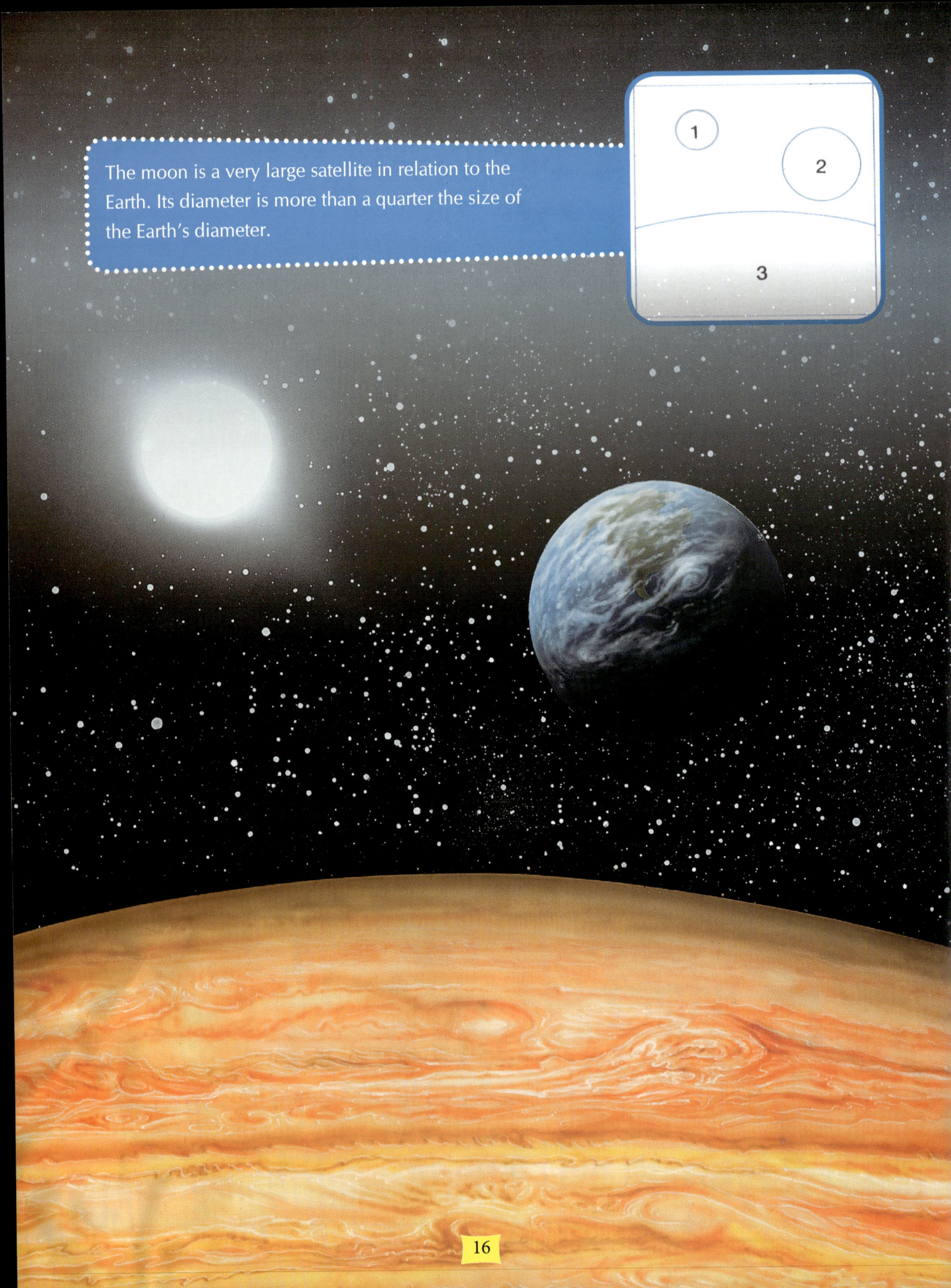

The moon is a very large satellite in relation to the Earth. Its diameter is more than a quarter the size of the Earth's diameter.

Movements of the Earth

Earth, like all the bodies in the Solar System, is trapped by the gravitational force between itself and the Sun. This force causes the Earth to travel in an orbit around the Sun, taking a year to complete each trip. The journey around the Sun is one of the reasons for the changing seasons on Earth. The distance from the Earth to the Sun varies very little along the orbit; it averages 150 million kilometres. This distance is so great that the light of the Sun takes more than eight minutes to reach the Earth.

In the polar regions, the Sun never sets in summer. Towards midnight it nears the horizon, but does not set completely. The 'midnight sun' can be seen within the Arctic and Antarctic circles.

Night and Day

While orbiting the Sun, the Earth also spins on its own axis, turning once each day. This is why we have day and night. The Earth rotates towards the east, so on Earth we see the Sun move from east to west every day.
At night the whole night sky seems to move from east to west. The stars move in the same way as the Sun.

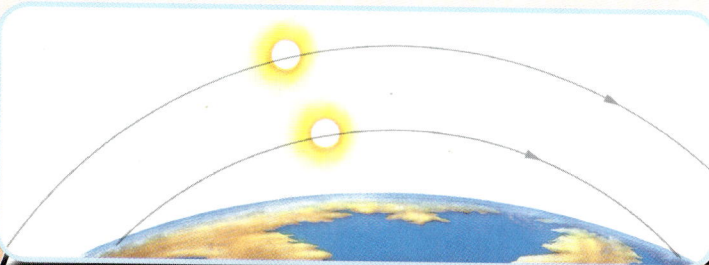

The Sun does not always rise or set at the same point on the horizon. In summer it follows a higher part in the sky than in winter.

The whole night sky seems to turn in the opposite direction to the rotation of the Earth. The Earth's axis of rotation points towards the North Star. If we look at this star in the northern hemisphere, we can see all the stars turning together around it, traveling east-to-west. There is no bright south star in the southern hemisphere, but the stars seem to move the opposite way, around one particular point in the southern sky. This point is known as the celestial south pole.

The Changing Seasons

We are used to seeing the seasons change through the year from spring to summer, autumn and winter. The Seasons are caused by the tilt of the Earth on its axis, and the movement of the Earth around the Sun.

The Solstices

The north end of the axis of rotation of the Earth points almost directly at the North Star. But, the Earth's axis is not at right angles to the plane of its orbit around the Sun. So while the Earth is travelling around the Sun, there is one particular moment in the year when the Sun reaches a high point above the Earth's equator. At another moment, six months later, the Sun is exactly the same distance below the equator. These two moments are called **solstices.** They occur on 21 June and 21 December, and they mark the beginning of summer and winter. The **equinoxes**, which occur around 21 March and 23 September, mark the beginning of the other two seasons, spring and autumn.

The Earth at the beginning of summer in the northern hemisphere and winter in the southern hemisphere (left). Six months later, it will be winter in the northern hemisphere and summer in the southern hemisphere (right).

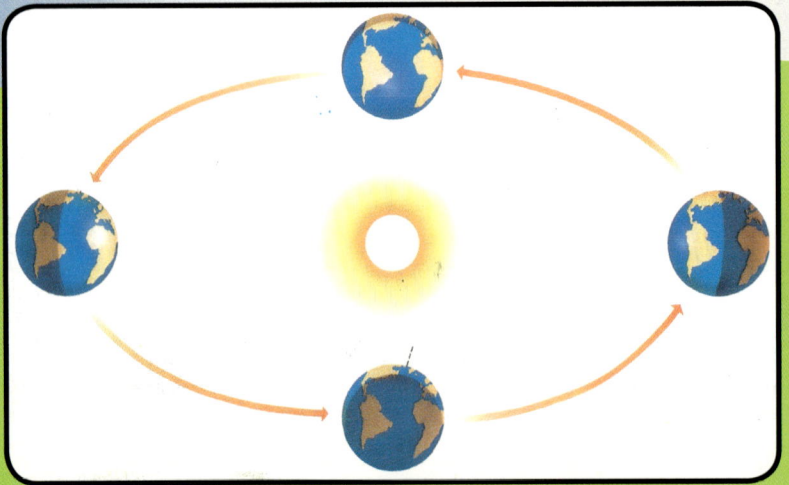

The Earth's axis always points towards the North Star as it orbits the Sun.

This picture shows the position of the Sun at the same time in the morning every two weeks for a year. In summer [1] the Sun is high, which means that the days are longer than the nights. In winter the opposite is true because the Sun is lower [2]. The movement of the Earth around the Sun does not always follow an exact pattern, so at sometimes of the year the Sun seems to move ahead slightly [3] and at others it seems to lag behind [4]. This means that the Sun's positions trace the shape of a figure eight, called an analemma.

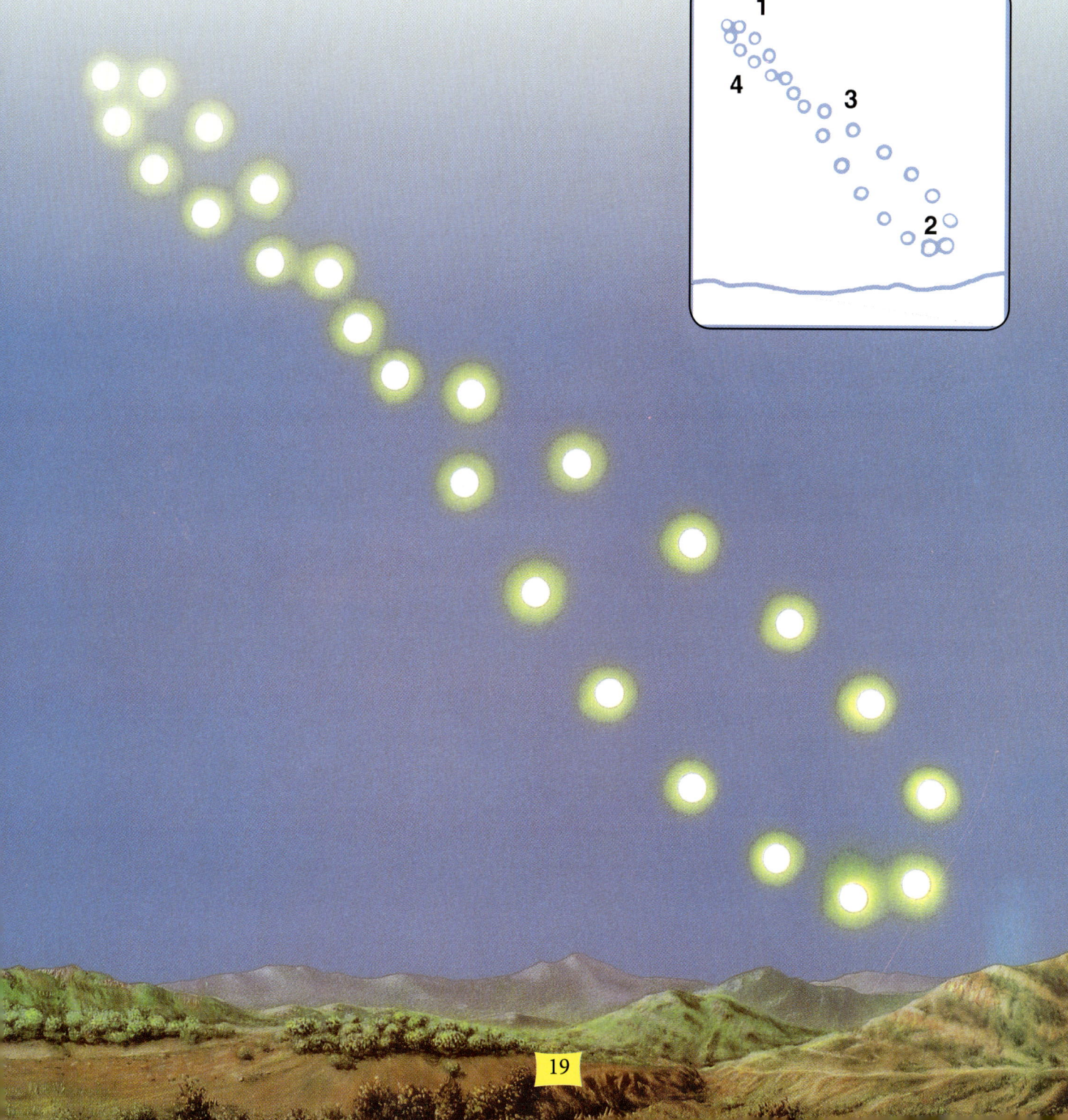

The Formation of the Earth

The Earth was formed along with the rest of the Solar System at the same time as the Sun. About 5000 million years ago, a cloud of interstellar matter (the gas and dust between the stars) from our galaxy began to contract and press together under its own gravitational pull.

The Earth's Core

In the centre of the cloud the Sun **condensed.** The rest of the cloud formed a flat disc that began to spin around the Sun. The **matter** that the cloud contained gradually condensed into **granules** that collided with each other and formed bodies, some as large as a kilometr in diameter. The **core** of the Earth was formed from the collision of several of these bodies, and attracted some of the matter near it. This is how Earth and all the other planets were created. The formation of the Sun and planets took several hundred million years. The newly-formed Earth was very different from the one we know today. A fierce heat was produced by disintegrating radioactive matter and the continuous bombardment of bodies falling on the Earth. This caused the centre of the Earth to melt. The most dense matter settled towards the centre of the planet where it formed a core of iron and nickel. At the same time, the lighter matter floated towards the surface and formed a **mantle** of molten rock made up of **silicates**. As the planet cooled, the surface crust of solid rock was created. This rock formed the ocean beds and all the **continents.**

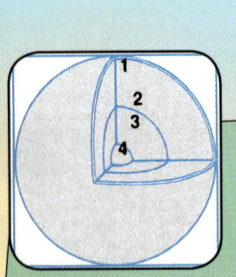 

Beneath the thin crust of the Earth [1] there are several layers that become gradually denser and hotter. The mantle [2] is made of molten rock, while the outer core is made up of the heaviest elements such as iron, which is in a liquid form [3]. In the inner core [4] the iron is solid because of very high pressure from the outer layers of the Earth.

Meteors bombarding the Earth (A) heated it until it melted (B). The heaviest elements sank (C) and came together in the central core (D).

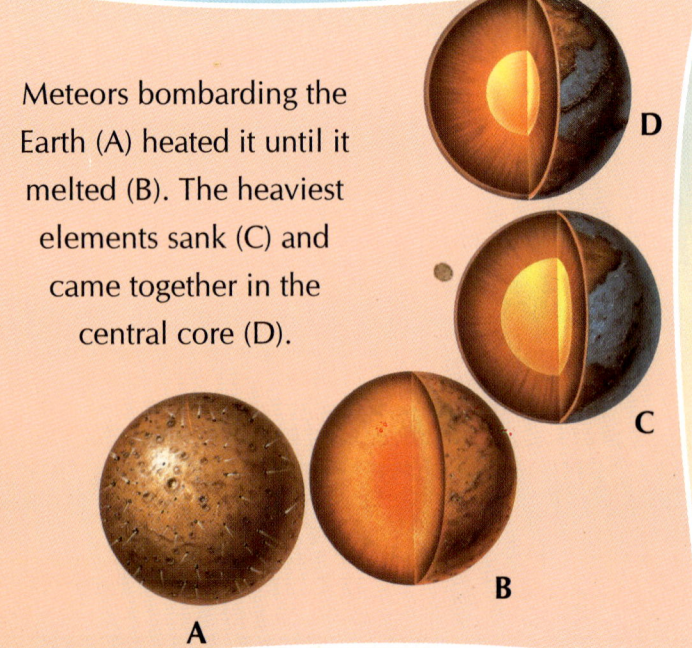

20

Bombarded by Meteorites

When the Solar system was young and the planets had only just formed, **inter-planetary space** was littered with material that had not come together to make planets. Many bodies fell on the newly-formed Earth, drawn by its gravitational pull. This continuous bombardment contributed to the heating and fusion of the Earth's matter.

Meteors and Meteorites

Inter-planetary space is now much cleaner. The bodies that still fall on the Earth are usually small granules of inter-planetary dust that are swept along by the Earth in its journey around the sun. These granules of dust enter the atmosphere at high speeds, become very hot and vaporize, forming **meteors** or shooting stars. Some granules may be big enough to survive the journey through the atmosphere without being burned up. They reach the ground, to become **meteorites,** rocks that have fallen from the sky. When meteorites are really large, they form craters in the Earth's surface where they have fallen. There are several craters on the Earth today that were caused by meteorites.

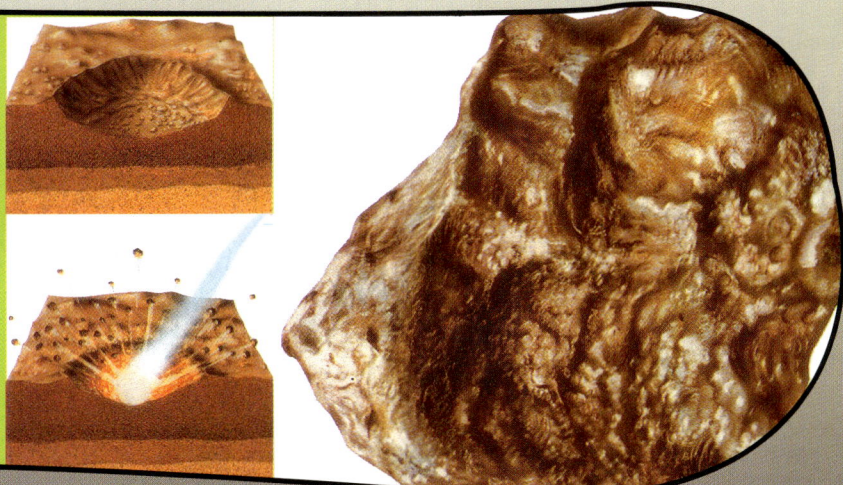

Meteorites that reach the Earth at high speeds can cause craters similar to those we can see on the Moon.

This crater in Arizona, USA, was made by a large meteorite. These craters are often eroded away in a few million years, a relatively short time compared with the age of the Earth.

The space between the planets is not empty. Inter-planetary debris of all sizes and shapes is found there: asteroids, comets, dust and even gas. Most asteroids have gathered in an area of the Solar System called the asteroid belt, between Mars and Jupiter. The gravitational influence of Jupiter, the largest planet of the Solar System, has prevented the asteroids from coming together to form a planet.

THE EARTH'S CRUST

The surface layer of the Earth is known as its **crust**. The crust's structure is very varied. Under the continents it is about 40 kilometres thick, but beneath the oceans it can be as little as 6 kilometres thick. This is only about one-thousandth of the Earth's radius.

Volcanoes on Io, a satellite of Jupiter, shoot sulphurous material to great heights.

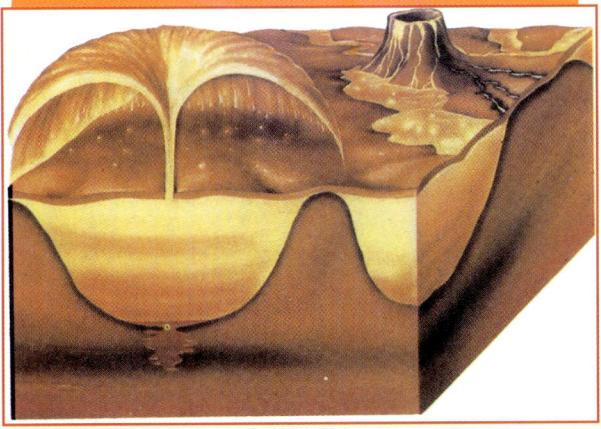

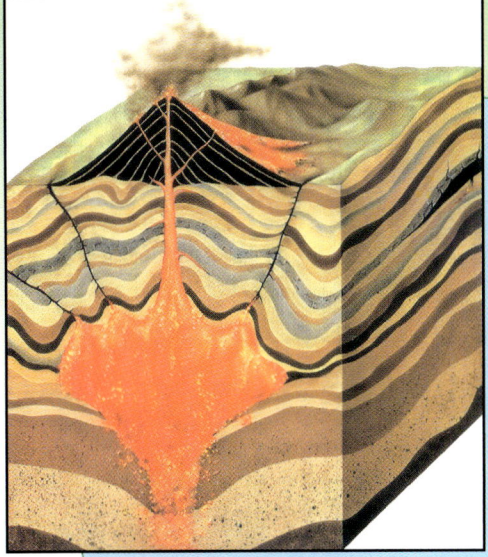

Where molten rock, or magma, rises to the Earth's surface, volcanoes are created. The areas of the world where there is a great deal of volcanic activity also tend to suffer from frequent earthquakes.

The Earth's crust is much thinner at the bottom of the oceans [1] than on the continents [2]. The plates that support the continents float on the mantle [3] and move around slowly, pushed by currents of magma. The folds in the crust produce mountain ranges. The highest mountains on Earth are the Himalayas. These rise more than 8 kilometres above sea level. They were formed when the plate containing the Indian subcontinent pushed against the Asiatic plate.

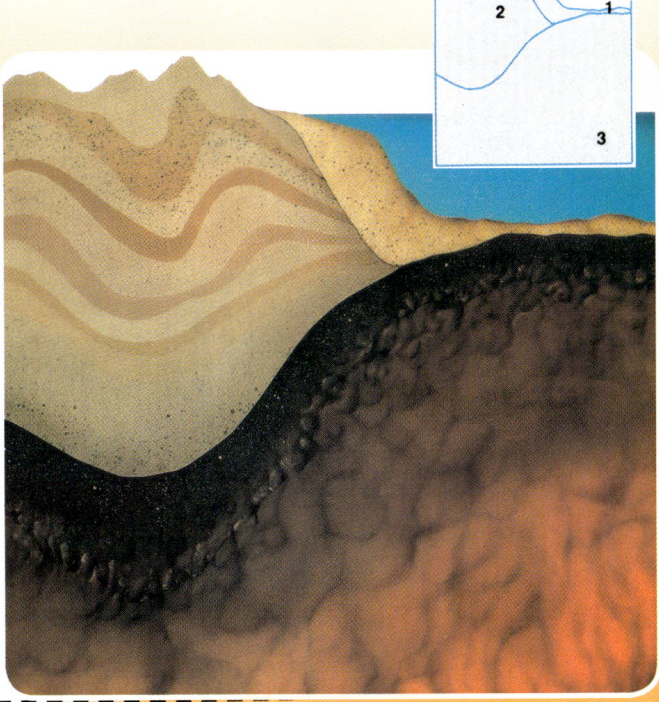

Earth's Magnetism

The Earth has a fairly intense magnetic field. Think of it as a huge magnetized bar inside the Earth's core, placed slightly off cent and tilted away from the Earth's axis of rotation. The magnetic north of the Earth is near the geographic North Pole, although they are not in exactly the same place. The distance between these two points is about 1000 kilometres. Magnetic South and South Pole are a similar distance apart.

Using a Compass

You can use a compass to find the North Magnetic Pole. A compass is a magnetized needle that can swing freely. It always points to magnetic north, and therefore tells us which direction is north. How did the Earth's magnetic field come about? The core acts like a giant electromagnet. In an electromagnet, electric currents flowing through a coil of wire produce a magnetic field. In the Earth, electric currents flow through its metallic core, which is made up mainly of iron and nickel. These currents produce the Earth's magnetic field.

The Magnetosphere

The Earth's magnetic field extends into space. The part of inter-planetary space where the Earth's magnetism has an effect is called the **magnetosphere**. The charged particles that continuously stream from the Sun bounce off the magnetic field when they reach the Earth's magnetosphere.

The stream of charged particles in the solar wind are deflected by the Earth's magnetic field when they reach the Earth's magnetosphere. Most particles flow around the Earth, but some are trapped in two belt-like areas around the Earth known as the Van Allen belts. They contain a large number of highly charged particles.

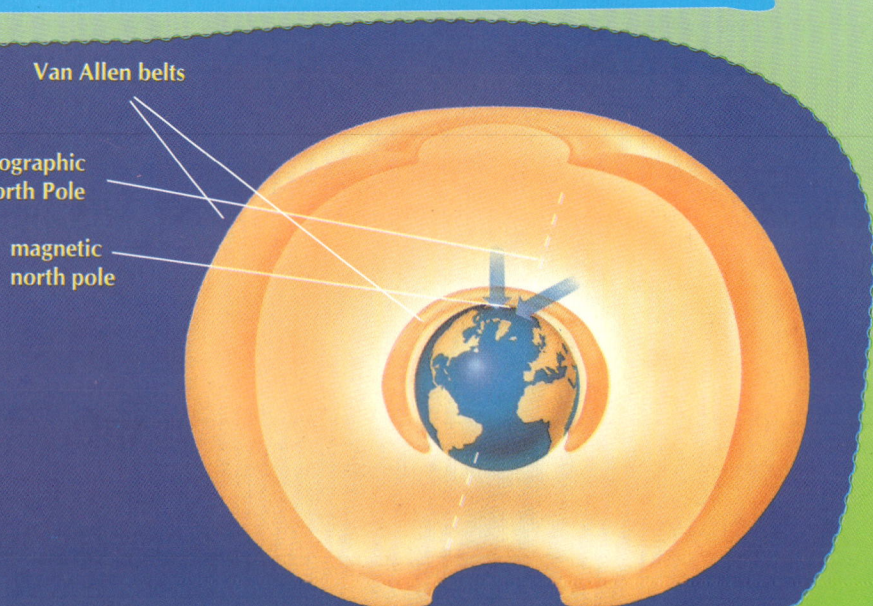

Some high-energy particles emitted by the Sun can reach the Earth's atmosphere, near the poles. When they strike the atmosphere, the atoms of atmospheric gas give off brightly-coloured lights which can be seen high up in the sky. The lights are known as the Aurora Borealis, or the northern lights near the North Pole. Near the South Pole they are called the aurora australis or southern lights. They can usually be seen only from latitudes close to either pole.

THE FORMATION OF THE ATMOSPHERE

The Earth is surrounded by a layer of gases that we call the atmosphere. The Earth's present-day atmosphere is not at all like the atmosphere that was formed at the same time as the planet. When the Sun was newly formed, it emitted an intense stream of particles which completely swept away the original layer of gases around the planets near the Sun. Today's atmosphere is the result of intense volcanic action during the first phases of the Earth's development. The volcanoes threw up large quantities of carbon dioxide, steam and other gases.

The Oceans

As the Earth cooled, the steam condensed into liquid, and formed the oceans. A great deal of carbon dioxide was dissolved in the sea water. From there, it passed into the shells of the millions of sea creatures that fell to the sea bed when they died. Their remains turned into present-day limestone.

Life on Earth

The nitrogen in our atmosphere comes from the ammonia-loaded gases given off by ancient volcanoes. These gases were broken down by **ultraviolet light** from the Sun. The oxygen was produced by the evolution of life on Earth. Green algae in the oceans was one of the first forms of life to appear. It absorbed carbon dioxide from the atmosphere and produced a large quantity of oxygen.

The Earth's atmosphere consists mainly of nitrogen from the original volcanoes, and of oxygen produced by the first plants.

Mercury has no atmosphere because of its small size and it is close to the Sun.

Venus has a dense atmosphere that consists mainly of carbon dioxide. This traps the heat from the Sun which raises the surface temperature.

Mars has a thin atmosphere composed largely of carbon dioxide with traces of oxygen and water vapour.

The atmosphere is the gaseous layer surrounding our planet. If we compare the Earth with other planets we can see that the Earth's atmosphere is rather special: mostly nitrogen and oxygen. Carbon dioxide is the main gas on Venus and Mars, and hydrogen the most common gas on Jupiter and Saturn. Our present atmosphere is the result of the conditions under which the Earth was formed and of the evolution of life on the planet.

Influences on the Earth

The Earth is not isolated from the rest of the universe. It is influenced by other stars, and this influence is easily seen. The star that has the greatest influence over the Earth is the Sun.

The Earth is constantly showered by meteorites. Most of these burn up completely in the atmosphere, producing shooting stars. Many of these are created when the Earth crosses the orbit of a comet.

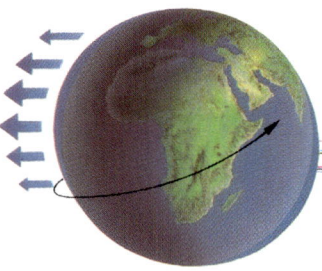

Food and Energy

The Sun makes it possible for life to develop and thrive and for human beings to survive on Earth. Sunlight is vital for life. The **food chain** of all living things begins with the Sun as its source of energy, because plants need the energy of sunlight to grow. Nearly all the forms of energy that humans use (except nuclear energy) come from the Sun, including energy from wind and water and from fossil fuels such as coal and petrol.

Ocean Tides

Apart from this close relationship with the Sun, the Earth is also linked with other bodies of the Solar System, especially the Moon. The Moon is the main cause of the Earth's ocean tides. The level of the sea rises and falls in a cycle that is repeated more or less twice a day. The tides cause the rotation of the Earth to slow down gradually, and this in turn causes a very slow lengthening of the day.

The Moon

The Moon's gravitational attraction is strongest on the side of the planet nearest to it. The water closest to it bulges towards the Moon, while the water on the opposite side of Earth forms another bulge. This results in the tides; the rising and falling of the level of the sea.

The Earth [1] has a very close relationship with the Sun [2] and the Moon [3]. The Earth and all the planets were formed along with the Sun, the central star of our Solar System. From the Sun the Earth receives all the energy it needs to sustain its animal and plant life. The Moon is the main cause of the ocean tides.

LIFE BEYOND THE EARTH?

Earth is the only place in the universe where we are certain that life exists. It is possible that the universe is full of life, but at the moment no **extraterrestrial** life has been found. Scientists have not been able to prove that any star other than the Sun, has a system of planets around it.

Why did life begin?

In our Solar System, there is probably no life anywhere other than on Earth. Why has life developed on Earth and not on other planets? Life, as we know it, cannot begin to develop without liquid water or mild temperatures.

A Delicate Balance

Life exists on Earth because of a delicate balance between the orbit of the planet and the conditions on its surface.

As it has developed, life has also gradually altered these conditions. Our atmosphere contains oxygen and lacks carbon dioxide as a result of the presence of life on the Earth. Today, humans can alter this delicate balance by choice or by accident. It is our responsibility to keep the Earth habitable.

Mars is an example of what Earth would be like if it had been further away from the Sun. Most of the water on Mars is in the form of ice at the polar caps.

On Venus, which is closer to the Sun than Earth, the temperature is very high due to the greenhouse effect. The carbon dioxide in the atmosphere on Venus lets solar light reach and warm the planet, but it does not allow the heat to escape.

At the moment, Earth seems to be the only planet in the Solar System where there is life. Mars, the planet that seemed most likely to support life, was explored by two viking inter-planetary probes [1] that photographed its surface and took samples of the soil [2] to analyse for living organisms. Nothing was found and scientists do not expect to find new forms of life in future explorations.

THE FUTURE OF THE EARTH

The Earth is a planet which has the right conditions for developing and sustaining life. We are not sure that these conditions will continue for many more years. Human activity can change the conditions on earth forever. An accident or a full-scale nuclear war could poison the Earth's surface for many thousands of years or cause the devastation of a nuclear winter. The increased level of carbon dioxide in the atmosphere has caused a greenhouse effect. This could lead to an increase in Earth's temperature which could turn it into an inferno like Venus. The breaking up of the ozone layer could also leave the Earth unprotected from the ultraviolet rays of the Sun.

The End of Energy

Astronomically, the future of the Earth is very clear. Earth is strongly affected by the Sun. In about 5,000 million years, the Sun's energy will start to run out, and it will change drastically to become a **red giant.** The surface of the Sun will swell enormously and swallow up the nearest planets. This will be the end of Earth as a habitable planet. But this is not an immediate threat. There are still 5,000 million years to go!

About 5,000 million years ago, the Sun was formed (A). The stability of the Sun in its present phase (B) has made life on Earth possible. When the Sun becomes a red giant (C), life on Earth will end. Finally, the Sun will shrink as it runs out of nuclear fuel, changing into a **white dwarf** (B).

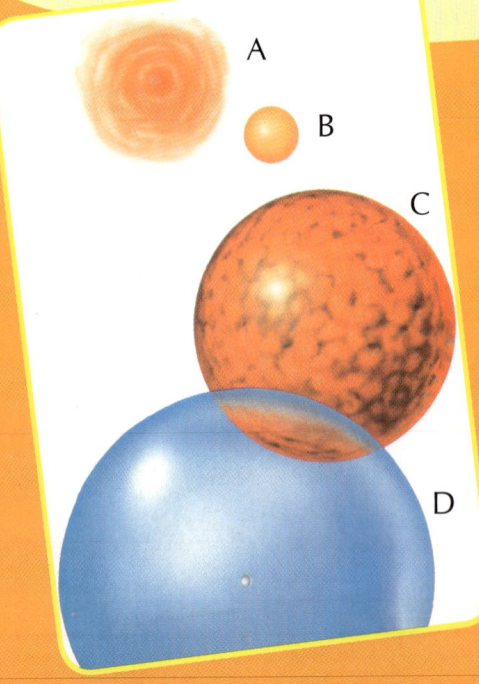

From our Story-book

You must have heard captivating stories from your elders describing the origin of the world. The Finnish epic poem Kalevala, the Chinese story of Pangu or the Indian Brahmanda Purana gives an exciting picture and tells us about the hidden meaning behind the formation of the Universe. But, remember always go by encyclopedia's. Interestingly, they give away accurate information.

Swollen Sun

In 5,000 million year's time, the Sun will swell and change into a red giant. From the Earth, the Sun [1] will appear as a huge reddish sphere that will cover almost the entire sky. The enormous rise in temperature will make the Earth's oceans evaporate [2]. Earth will become uninhabitable. It may even be swallowed up entirely by the Sun.

ACTIVITY: MAKE A SUNDIAL

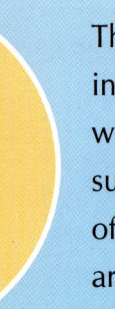

The movement of the Sun tells us what time of the day it is and influences what we do. Until only a relatively short time ago, there was no clock more perfect than the Sun. Today clocks work with such precision that they even show up the slightest irregularities of the Sun's **'movement'** (it is, in fact, the movement of the Earth around the Sun that is irregular).

Sundials were the earliest clocks. The principle behind the sundial is very simple. The Earth rotates so the Sun moves from our view and seems to turn around the Earth's axis, completing one revolution (360 degrees) every 24 hours. If we line up an arm or stick with the angle of the Earth's axis, its shadow will turn in exactly the same way as the Sun appears to and every hour the shadow will travel 15 degrees. The shadow can be projected on to a flat surface, or dial, at right angles to the arm. Lines 15 degrees apart are drawn on the dial so that each line represents an hour.

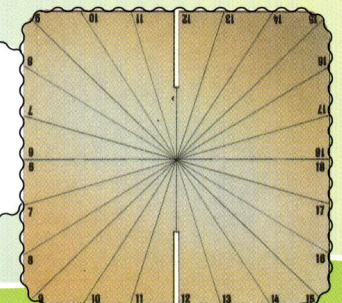

The triangular part is the arm of the sundial. The dial is the rectangular part and has two faces, one for winter and the other for summer. Both faces have the hours marked out from 6 to 18 hours (6am to 6pm).

How to make your own sundial

You will need two square pieces of cardboard which are 30cm wide, a ruler, a compass, a protractor, a pen, and a pair of scissors.

1. Take one of the pieces of card and cut it in half diagonally to form a triangle.
2. Using the scissors, make a slit on the longest side of the triangle as shown.
3. Next, take the second sheet of card and using your ruler, protractor and pen, divide the square into 24 equal parts.
4. Now fold the square in half to form a rectangle and draw a number on each part from 6 to 18.
5. Using the scissors, make a slit half way along the folded rectangle next to the number 12.
6. Fit the two pieces of card together to make your sundial complete.
7. When the Sun is shining, take your compass and your sundial outside. Use your compass to line up the bottom of the triangle with the north-south line on your compass.

Planets and Satellites

Did you know that our Solar system is called the Milky Way and there are eight more planets that accompany the Earth in its scrupulous journey? Go through the specifics in this chapter and be thrilled as you read the most interesting facts coupled with new discoveries as well as the mass satellite expeditions blasted into space.

The Planets of the Solar System

The Earth is a small planet which revolves around the Sun, one of the 100 billion stars in our galaxy. Other planets, eight in all, move around the Sun, captives of its gravitational pull. Almost all the planets have satellites that orbit around them. This group, composed of the Sun, the planets and their satellites, together with a multitude of smaller bodies, principally asteroids and comets, makes up the **Solar System.**

The four planets closest to the Sun (Mercury, Venus, Earth, and Mars, in order of increasing distance) have similar characteristics and for this they are called the **terrestrial planets**. They are small, rocky bodies, with a relatively high density, and have few or no satellites, The four following planets (Jupiter, Saturn, Uranus, and Neptune) are called the **giant planets**. They are more in their original form than the terrestrial planets and consist mostly of gases.

Pluto doesn't fit in this category. It is the most distant planet, and the smallest.

The solar system was created out of interstellar material, in whose centre a star, the Sun, was condensed (A). The rest of the material began to spin around it, condensing into different celestial bodies (B). The different gravitational pulls of these celestial bodies resulted in the formation of the planets and the satellites(C).

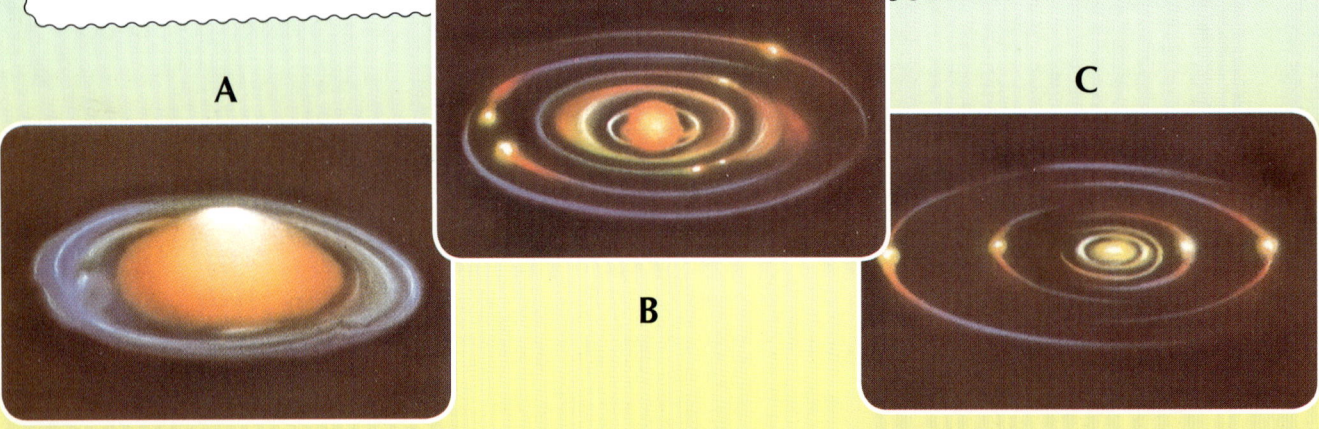

From left to right in the illustration: the small, rocky planets—Mercury, Venus, Earth, Mars; the giant, gaseous planets—Jupiter, Saturn, Uranus, Neptune; and tiny Pluto.

The Solar System was created five billion years ago. A cloud of interstellar dust and gas began to come together due to the effects of its own gravitational pull: the first step toward the forming of the Solar System. In its centre, the Sun was formed [1] and afterwards the interstellar material condensed into other celestial bodies "trapped" by the gravitational pull [2]. The successive condensation of material and the bombardment of meteorites [3] formed the early Solar System.

Mercury, the closest to the Sun

Because it is so close to the Sun, Mercury is a difficult planet to observe. It can only be observed for a maximum of two hours at dusk, after sunset, or before sunrise. A great deal of what we know about Mercury comes from the exploration carried out by the *Mariner 10* interplanetary space probe in the year 1974 and 1975 when it circled the planet three times.

Mercury's orbit around the Sun distinguishes it from the other planets by two peculiarities. For one thing, its ecliptic plane is more inclined than the majority of planets. Another thing is that it has a very **elliptical** orbit. When Mercury passes the **perihelion** (the point of the orbit when it is closest to the Sun), the distance to the Sun is less than two-third of the distance when it passes by the **aphelion** (the point farthest from the Sun). Mercury is so close to the Sun that it receives six times more solar radiation than the Earth. As you can imagine, the temperature on its illuminated side is very high. Mercury's surface appears to be covered with craters similar to those of the Moon. The origin of these craters is the impact of meteorites of all sizes, which populated the Solar System when the planets finished forming, five billion years ago. Mercury's craters, like those of the Moon, have remained intact all this time, thanks to the absence of erosion, since Mercury has no **atmosphere.**

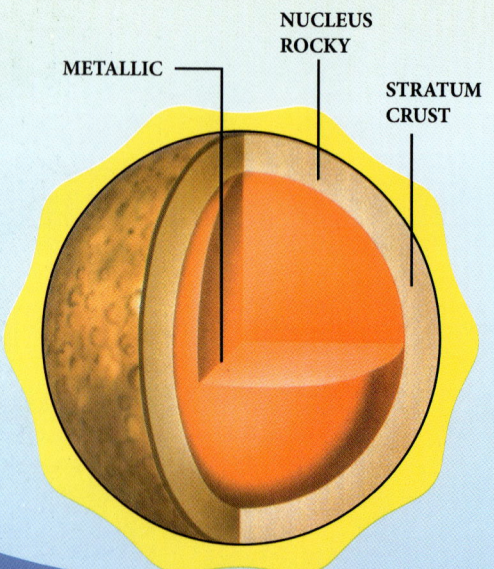

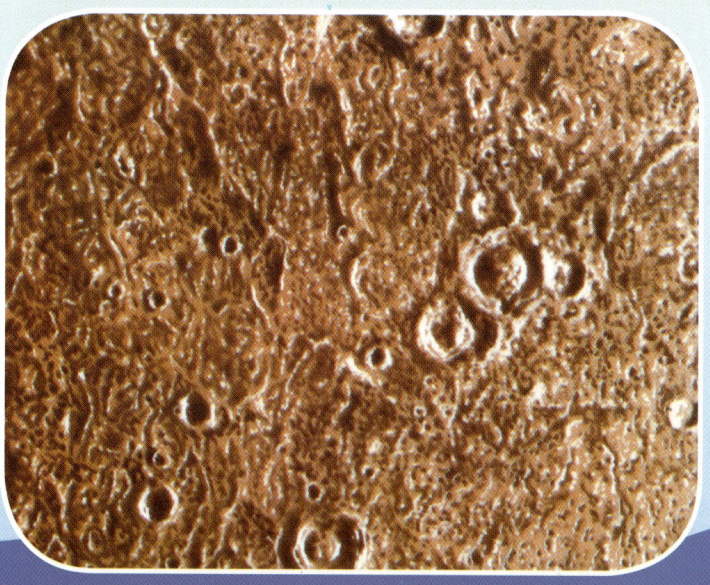

Mercury Facts

Average distance from the Sun: 36 million miles (58 million kilometres) (0.39 times that of Earth)
Length of year: 0.24 Earth years
Length of a day: 59 Earth days
Diameter: 3,032.4 miles (4,878 kilometres) (0.38 times that of Earth), Gravity: 0.37 times that of Earth
Satellites: none

Mercury's surface is similar to that of the Moon, since it has numerous craters caused by the impact of meteorites. The craters have been safe from erosion because Mercury has no atmosphere. The reason for this absence of atmosphere is that the force of the planet's gravitational pull is too weak to retain atmospheric gases.

Mercury is the planet closest to the Sun. Thanks to the information given to us by space probes, we know that its surface is arid and rocky and that it is furrowed with craters and mountain ranges. The light which Mercury receives from the Sun is six times more intense than the light which arrives at the Earth. During the day the temperature on Mercury exceeds 800°F (430°C).

Venus, forever covered by clouds

Venus is the planet that comes closest to the Earth, and shines very brightly in the sky. Because of its position near the Sun, it can only be seen for a few hours after sunset or before sunrise. Venus' size and distance from the Sun makes it seem very similar to the Earth. It was believed for a long time, before its characteristics were fully known, that the planet could sustain life. However, it was discovered that it has a surface temperature of 860°F (460°C), much higher than what it logically should be when taking into account its distance from the Sun. Why is the temperature so high? The answer lies in the atmosphere of Venus.

The atmosphere of Venus is very dense. Solar light can penetrate it and heat the planet's surface, but the heat emitted from the surface cannot escape through the atmosphere. It remains trapped on the planet. This is what is known as the *greenhouse effect*, which has converted Venus into an inferno of high temperature and pressure (about 100 times that of Earth). Venus' surface cannot be observed directly because the planet is permanently covered by a thick layer of clouds. Venus is a planet geologically alive and probably has active volcanoes. There are mountains higher than Everest on Venus, and land formations that remind us of the continents on Earth, rising above the average level of the planet. Among them are great depressions that may at one time have been ocean beds, which evaporated long ago.

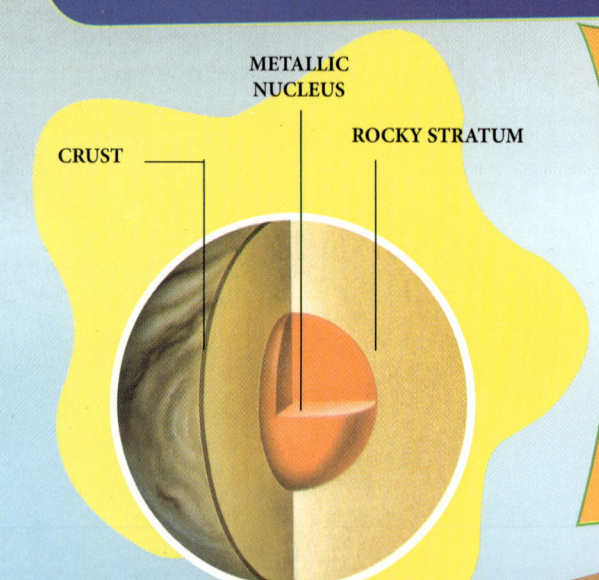

CRUST

METALLIC NUCLEUS

ROCKY STRATUM

Venus Facts
Average distance from the Sun: 67 million miles (108 million kilometres) (0.72 times that of Earth)
Length of year: 0.62 Earth years
Length of a day: 243 Earth days
Diameter: 7,519 miles (12,104 kilometres) (0.95 times that of Earth)
Gravity: 0.91 times that of Earth
Satellites: none

The Russian interplanetary probes, called Venera, landed on Venus' surface and were able to transmit a few images before being destroyed after several minutes by the enormous pressure and temperature on Venus. The images transmitted by the probes show flat terrain covered with rocks, worn down by Venus' atmosphere.

Venus [1] is the second planet from the Sun and the closest to the Earth [2]. It is covered by a thick layer of clouds, composed of carbon dioxide, which prevents observation of its surface.

Earth, the blue planet

Earth is the planet which we inhabit. We're used to living on it and it's hard for us to think of it as a planet. How is it seen from space? The first thing that stands out is its blue colour. A great deal of its surface is covered by water, forming oceans. It is the only planet where water exists in liquid form. Water is also found in the clouds in the atmosphere in the form of ice crystals, which gives them their characteristic white colour. The Earth's atmosphere, composed of nitrogen and oxygen, is another of this planet's peculiarities. Compared to Venus or Mars, the Earth's atmosphere at present has little carbon dioxide. What there was initially was dissolved in the sea water and consumed by the first forms of life which appeared on the Earth. These were green sea algae, which enriched the atmosphere with oxygen. Geologically, the Earth is a very active planet. The Earth's crust is divided into great plates, which are pushed by slow currents. Europe and America, which are on different plates, continue to separate a few centimetres each year. At the bottom of the Atlantic Ocean, where the crust is thinnest, a new crust is forming. In other regions of the Earth, the plates collide, resulting in earthquakes. The Earth is not an isolated planet. It possesses a satellite, the Moon, which stands out for its size. Its diameter is one-fourth the size of the Earth's.

Earth's crust is formed by large plates that "float" over its mantle. At the bottom of the Atlantic Ocean we find the Atlantic Dorsal, a great mountain range that separates the European and American plates.

Earth Facts
Average distance from the Sun: 93 million miles (150 million kilometres)
Diameter: 7,926.2 miles (12,104 kilometres)
Distance from the Earth to the Moon: 239,000 miles (384,400 kilometres)
Diameter of the Moon: 0.27 times that of the Earth
Gravity on the Moon: 0.17 that of the Earth
Satellites: 1

SOLID METALLIC NUCLEUS

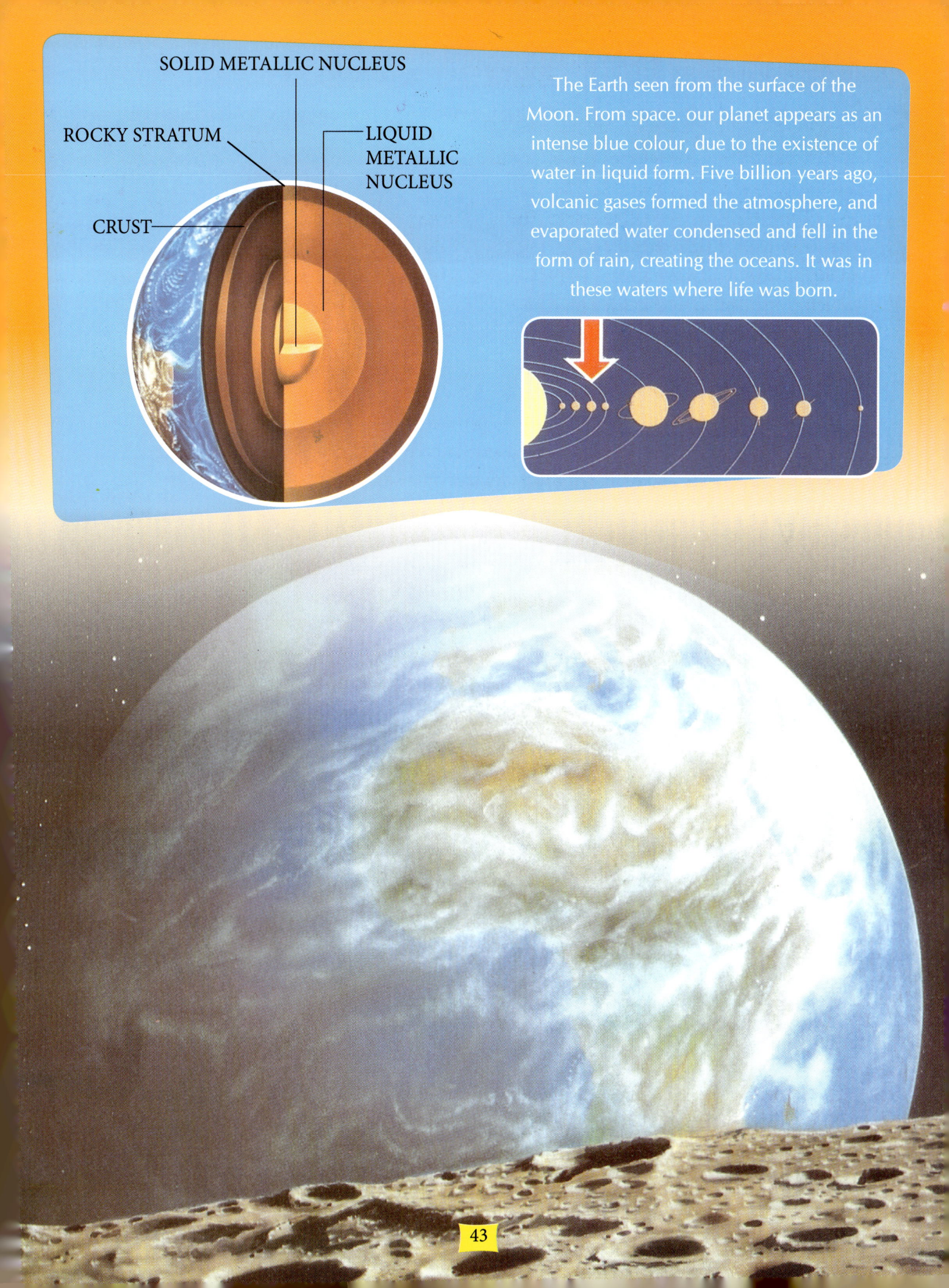

ROCKY STRATUM

LIQUID METALLIC NUCLEUS

CRUST

The Earth seen from the surface of the Moon. From space. our planet appears as an intense blue colour, due to the existence of water in liquid form. Five billion years ago, volcanic gases formed the atmosphere, and evaporated water condensed and fell in the form of rain, creating the oceans. It was in these waters where life was born.

Mars, the red planet

For a long time, it was thought that Mars, the red planet, was inhabited by extraterrestrial beings, the "martians," who had built an extensive network of "canals" on the planet's surface. It has been confirmed that there are no canals and that there has been no intelligent life on Mars. But the interest awakened about the planet has not subsided, and, after the Moon, it will probably be the next body in the Solar System to be visited by astronauts. Mars has been explored by interplanetary probes. The Viking probes, without doubt the most famous, landed on its surface in 1976.

There are indications that in the past, the planet was similar to the Earth, and had water flowing on its surface. At present, the only water that exists in Mars is in the form of ice in the polar caps, or as occasional morning frost. Mars' seasons are similar to the Earth's and the polar caps vary throughout the year. In the summer hemisphere, the extension of ice is less than in the other hemisphere. The situation is reversed after half a Martian year. Mars has a very thin atmosphere composed mainly of carbon dioxide. Each Martian year, the changing of the seasons brings on enormous dust storms.

There are big mountains on the surface of Mars. Mount Olympus is the highest, at 78,000 feet (25,000 m). It is an ancient volcano, much higher than any other mountain on Earth.

Mars' two satellites, Phobos and Deimos, are very small irregular bodies. Phobos has a diameter of about 15 miles (25 kilometres) and takes 8 hours to rotate around Mars. Deimos is even smaller.

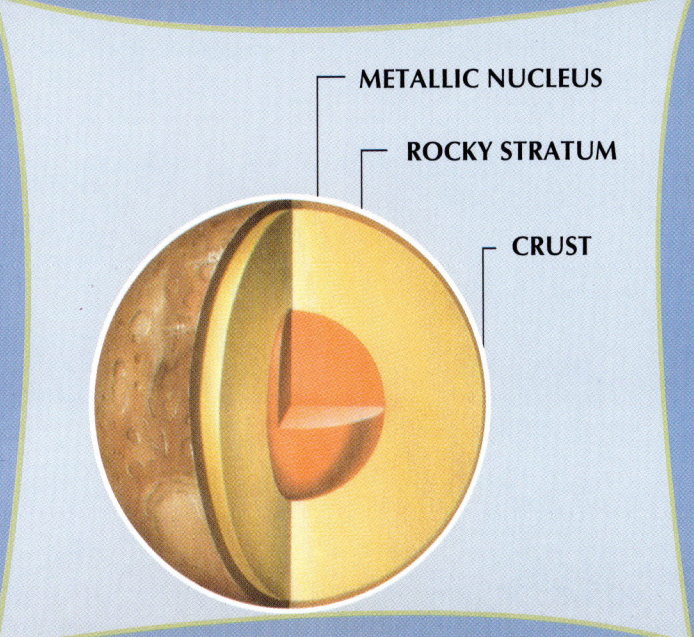

METALLIC NUCLEUS
ROCKY STRATUM
CRUST

A Viking interplanetary probe landed on Mars' surface. The images relayed by these probes show a reddish surface covered with pebbles, dust, and rocks in various sizes. The sky's colour is also red, due to the dust which floats in the air. The probes analyzed samples of the surface looking for signs of life, but the results were negative.

Mars Facts

Average distance from the Sun: 142 million miles (228 million kilometres) (1.52 times that of Earth)
Length of year: 1.88 Earth years
Length of a day: 1 Earth day
Diameter: 4,194 miles (6,787 kilometres) (0.53 times that of Earth), Gravity: 0.38 times that of Earth
Satellites: 2

Jupiter, the Giant Planet

Jupiter is the giant of the Solar System. Its diameter is ten times greater than the Earth's. Its gravitational pull is so high, that it slightly affects the movement of all the other planets, and is capable of diverting many comets that come close to its orbit.

Almost all of Jupiter's interior is composed of **hydrogen** (and some helium) in a liquid state, compressed by the enormous weight of the atmosphere above. Near the visible surface, where the pressure is less, the hydrogen passes into a gaseous state, forming the planet's atmosphere. The visible surface of the planet corresponds to the upper part of the clouds in the atmosphere, photographed by the interplanetary probes *Pioneer* and *Voyager* when they passed by Jupiter during their journey to the outer planets.

From the Earth, besides the structure of bands in the atmosphere, another detail of the atmosphere can be seen, the Great Red Spot situated in the southern hemisphere of the planet. The spot's reddish colour is produced by the compounds of nitrogen on Jupiter. In addition to its big family of satellites, Jupiter has a very thin ring formed by a multitude of particles, fairly close to the planet's upper cloud deck.

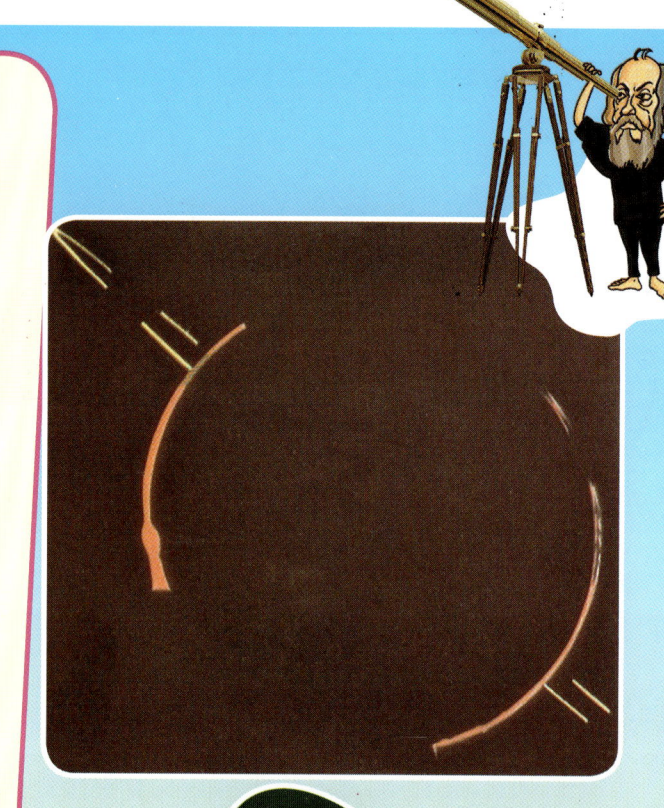

On the Voyager probe's travels to the outer planets, it captured images of Jupiter's dark side, where a thin ring surrounding the planet can be seen.

Jupiter's upper atmosphere is composed of a series of light and dark bands which represent higher and lower cloud layers.

LIGHT BANDS

DARK BANDS

GASEOUS ATMOSPHERE

LIQUID MOLECULAR HYDROGEN

METALLIC HYDROGEN NUCLEUS

ROCKY NUCLEUS

JUPITER FACTS

Average distance from the Sun: 483 million miles (778 million kilometres) (5.20 times Earth's)

Length of year: 12 Earth years

Length of a day: 10 Earth hours

Diameter: 88,736 miles (142,800 kilometres) (11.2 times that of Earth)

Gravity: 2.6 times that of Earth

Satellites: 4 big, 12 small

Rings: 1

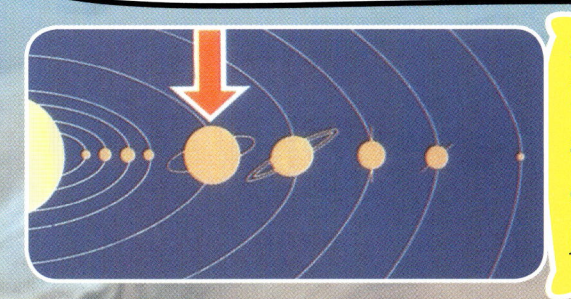

Most noticeable on Jupiter's surface is the Great Red Spot, [1] an immense whirlwind formed in the atmosphere with characteristics resembling those of cyclones on Earth. In the illustration, you can also see Jupiter's two principal satellites: Io [2] and Europa [3]

Jupiter's Satellites

Jupiter has a family of numerous satellites. At present, 16 are known. Among those, the four largest stand out: Io, Europa, Ganymede, and Callisto. They are called the *Galilean satellites* because they were discovered by Galileo when he observed Jupiter with a telescope. After the Moon, the Galilean satellites are the most famous in the Solar System. With a small telescope they can easily be observed from the Earth. They look like faint points of light lined up on one or both sides of Jupiter. The Galilean satellites were explored in detail by the *Voyager* probes, which obtained impressive images of all of them. Io, the closest of the four to Jupiter, is intense reddish-orange in colour and its surface is covered by sulphur compounds. Europa, the satellite next closest to Jupiter, has a very smooth, bright surface, covered by ice, and furrowed by a network of dark cracks. Ganymede is the largest satellite of the Solar System, even larger than Mercury. Its surface is quite varied, showing dark and light areas. Some craters stand out because of their whiteness, and were produced by meteorites that broke through the superficial layer of ice and dust.

Callisto is the farthest of the Galilean satellites.
Besides the four Galilean satellites, Jupiter has a multitude of small satellites. Some of them are most likely asteroids captured by Jupiter's gravitational pull.

Io has numerous volcanoes, which shoot material more than 60 miles (100 kilometres). This volcanic activity is caused by Jupiter's gravitational pull.

A comparison between Earth and the Moon with the size of the Galilean satellites, from left to right, Ganymede, Callisto, Io, and Europa. The Galilean satellites, with the exception of Europa, are larger than the Moon.

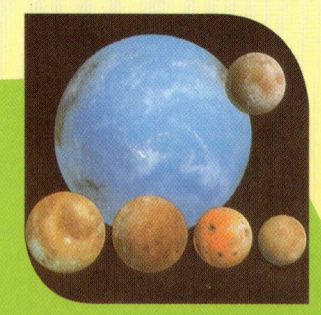

Europa has an extraordinary smooth surface, rather like an immense billiard ball. Under the surface of ice, it is believed that there could be a layer of liquid water, just like the Earth's Arctic Ocean.

Jupiter [1] has 16 satellites. They can be divided into three groups: an exterior group, the four Galilean satellites, and a group of satellites inside Jupiter's ring. The four Galilean satellites are : Io [2], the satellite closest to the planet and comparable in size to the Moon, Europa [3], with its smooth covering layer of ice, Ganymede [4], the largest satellite in the Solar System; and Callisto [5], the moon whose surface contains the most craters.

Saturn, a spectacular planet

Saturn's magnificent rings make this planet unmistakable. Even with a small telescope it is possible to see the little disk of Saturn surrounded by its rings. Saturn seems so small when seen from the Earth because it is almost twice as far away as Jupiter. In reality, the two planets are similar in size, although Saturn is slightly smaller. What makes Saturn stand out is its low density: it is the only planet in the Solar System less dense than water. If we were to put Saturn in a bathtub full of water, it would float! The problem is finding a bathtub big enough. Saturn is the planet with the most satellites. It has a total of 23, many of them extraordinarily small, discovered by **Voyager** probes when they passed close to Saturn. The biggest and most interesting of these satellites is Titan.

Compare the sizes of Titan, Rhea, Iapetus, Dione, and Tethys with those of the Earth and the Moon.

The surface of Mimas is partially covered by the crater Herschel, which was formed as a result of a tremendous impact which almost shattered the satellite into pieces.

Saturn Facts

average distance from the Sun: 887.14 million miles (1,424 million kilometres) (9.52 times Earth's)

Length of year: 29 Earth years

Length of a day: 10 Earth hours

Diameter: 74,978 miles (120,00 kilometres) (9.4 times that of Earth)

Gravity: 1.1 times that of Earth

Satellites: 5 big ones, 18 small

Rings: 3 major divisions

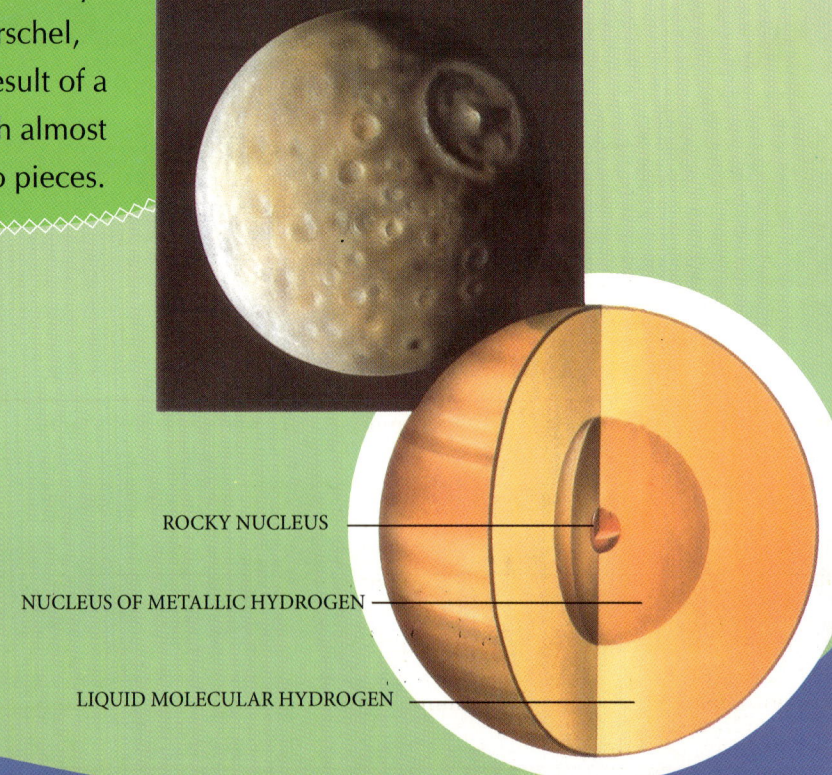

ROCKY NUCLEUS

NUCLEUS OF METALLIC HYDROGEN

LIQUID MOLECULAR HYDROGEN

Titan has a considerable atmosphere formed for the most part of nitrogen and methane, which prevent its surface from being seen. It is believed that the methane on Titan may play a similar role to that of water on the Earth. It could be present in solid or liquid form on the surface and in the form of a gas in the atmosphere. Titan is one of the bodies in the Solar System that will be explored in the future to see if some form of life inhabits the satellite using methane as the basis of life instead of water.

The other four large satellites (Rhea, Iapetus, Dione, and Tethys) have diametres of about 650 miles (1,000 kilometres) with an appearance similar to the Galilean satellites of Jupiter.

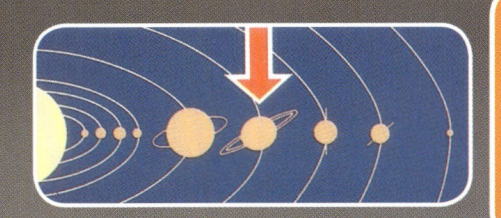

Saturn [1], with its system of rings, is the most spectacular planet of the Solar System. It also has the greatest number of satellites [23]. In the illustration, you can see Tethys [2], and Dione [3], two of the most important satellites. Mimas [4] stands out because of its crater.

Saturn's Rings

Saturn's Rings

All of the giant planets, Jupiter, Saturn, Uranus, and Neptune have rings. But none of them compares with the rings of Saturn. Without doubt, these are the most spectacular and most impressive show in the Solar System. Saturn's rings extend from close to the surface to more than twice the radius of the planet [about 87,000 miles (140,000 kilometres)].

You can see them easily from Earth with a small telescope, although every 15 years they stop being visible. It is then while in its orbit around the Sun, Saturn's position is such that its rings present themselves edge-on. The rings are so thin that when this happens, they cannot be seen from the Earth.

The ring F owes its unusual braided form to the presence of small satellites, called shepherd satellites, next to the ring.

The most brilliant ring is B, which is separated from the A ring by the Cassini Division. Other fainter rings, C and D, are closer to Saturn.

For a long time it was known that Saturn's rings were not solid. They are formed by a large quantity of small particles (from the size of dust particles to the size of a small house) mostly composed of ice. They move around Saturn following circular paths lined up with the planet's equator. Some of the material remains dispersed, unable to form satellites due to its proximity to the planet.

From the Earth, three principal rings can be distinguished. The most exterior is *ring A,* which is separated from *ring B* by the Cassini Division, an empty space between both rings. Ring A has its own division, called Encke, which is much narrower than that of Cassini. Closer to Saturn's surface we *see C,* thinner than the others. The rings have turned out to be much more complex than was believed before they were explored by the *Voyager* probe. More rings have been discovered, in particular the *ring F*, formed by two or three braided thread, Each ring, is composed of thousands of very narrow rings, and not all the divisions are completely empty space. *Voyager's* images of Saturn's rings are reminiscent of an immense phonograph records.

Saturn's ring system is one of the most spectacular phenomena of the Solar System. The thickness of the different fringes or rings is only a few miles. Each ring is formed by a great number of ice particles, each probably with a rocky nucleus. The size of these particles ranges from a little more than a fraction of an inch to close to 30 feet. These celestial bodies rotate around the planet, following circular orbits above Saturn's equator. The planet's gravitational pull prevents the particles from grouping and forming a satellite too close to Saturn.

Uranus, the first discovered with a telescope

Situated at a distance from the Sun almost twice that of Saturn, we find Uranus. It is one of the giant planets, although not as big as Jupiter or Saturn. Uranus was unknown in ancient times, and was the first planet to be discovered with a telescope. In fact, it can be seen with the naked eye, but without a big telescope, you wouldn't be able to distinguish the planet's disk. One of Uranus' notable characteristics is that the planet's rotation axis lies on the plane of its orbit around the Sun. In this way, Uranus' poles successively line up towards the Sun every half a Uranian year (every 42 Earth years). The rest of the planets have their axes more or less perpendicular to the ecliptic plane.

Uranus' rings, discovered from the Earth, are very thin and dark. The Voyager interplanetary probe observed a total of 11 rings around Uranus when it passed by the planet.

Uranus' four major satellites each have diametres of slightly less than 1,000 miles. They are similar to Jupiter's Galilean satellites. From left to right and from above to below, are Ariel, Umbriel, Titania, and Oberon.

Uranus is also, next to Saturn, the first planet where rings were discovered. In 1977 five thin rings around Uranus were observed from the Earth, while Uranus was passing in front of a distant but very brilliant star, which briefly covered its light. Five satellites belonging to Uranus have been observed from the Earth, but little can be learned about them from such a great distance. *Voyager* observed them in detail and also discovered 10 new satellites.

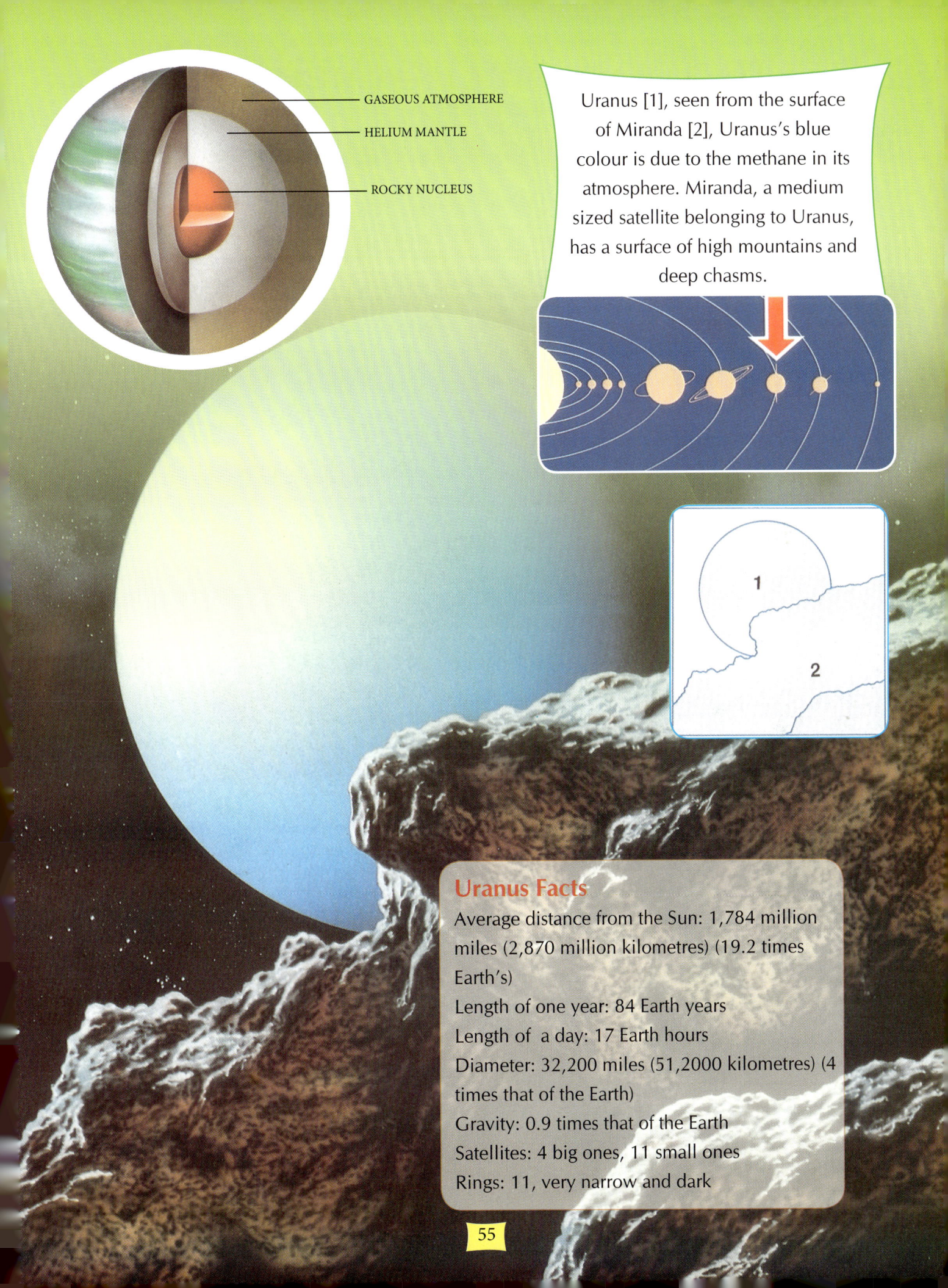

- GASEOUS ATMOSPHERE
- HELIUM MANTLE
- ROCKY NUCLEUS

Uranus [1], seen from the surface of Miranda [2], Uranus's blue colour is due to the methane in its atmosphere. Miranda, a medium sized satellite belonging to Uranus, has a surface of high mountains and deep chasms.

Uranus Facts

Average distance from the Sun: 1,784 million miles (2,870 million kilometres) (19.2 times Earth's)

Length of one year: 84 Earth years

Length of a day: 17 Earth hours

Diameter: 32,200 miles (51,2000 kilometres) (4 times that of the Earth)

Gravity: 0.9 times that of the Earth

Satellites: 4 big ones, 11 small ones

Rings: 11, very narrow and dark

Neptune, the farthest giant planet

Neptune was the first planet to be discovered. Neptune was the planet most recently visited by the *Voyager* interplanetary probe at the end of its twelve year journey through the Solar System. Neptune is so far away from us (30 times the distance from the Earth to the Sun) that it was poorly observed form the Earth. *Voyager's* images have revealed a planet with an intense blue colour, caused by the methane contained in its atmosphere, which is composed primarily of hydrogen and helium. Unlike Uranus, Neptune's atmosphere demonstrates great activity, with a structure of bands, a large dark spot similar to Jupiter's, and small white clouds. Neptune, like all the giant planets, has rings. From the Earth only incomplete pieces of the rings were seen, but *Voyager* revealed that the rings are complete with some parts brighter than others. From the Earth, the existence of two satellites, Nereid and Triton, was known. The *Voyager* probe discovered six more, all very small.

- GASEOUS ATMOSPHERE
- ROCKY NUCLEUS
- HELIUM MENTLE

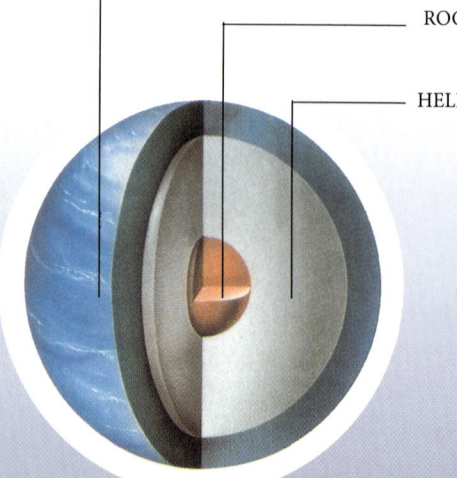

Triton and Nereid are Neptune's largest satellite. Triton is almost as big as the Moon and Nereid has a diameter of about 200 miles (300 kilometres).

Neptune Facts

Average distance from the Sun: 2,796 million miles (4,492 million kilometres) .(30 times Earth's)

Length of a year: 165 Earth years

Length of a day: 16 Earth hours

Diamete30,775 miles (48,700 kilometres) (3.8 times that of the Earth), Gravity: 1.2 times that of the Earth, Satellites: 2 big ones, 6 small ones

Rings: 4 narrow

Triton's surface has many narrow valleys, craters and peaks, and frozen lakes of volcanic origin.

Neptune [1] and its biggest satellite, Triton [2]. This satellite rotates in the reverse direction around Neptune, a unique case among the big satellites of the Solar System. It is possible that Triton was formed as an independent body and then was captured by Neptune.

ACTIVITY : A MODEL OF THE SOLAR SYSTEM

What does the Solar System look like from the outside? How are the planets separated from each other? The best way to answer these questions would be to construct a model of the Solar system and place objects where the Sun and the planets would be. You should use the same scale for the sizes of the objects, the distances between the planets, and their distances from the Sun. You can use a big ball, for example a basketball (approximately 25 centimetres or 10 inches in diameter) to represent the Sun. On this scale the terrestrial planets would have to be represented with heads of pins and marbles. Although you only want to construct a model of the Solar System's interior corresponding to the terrestrial planets, the distance at which you would have to put Mars—as you can see in the box below—would be very great. If you wanted to represent the whole Solar System using this scale, Jupiter would have a diameter of 2.5 centimetres (a big marble) and would be placed 143 metres from the Sun. Neptune 823 metres, and Pluto a distance of more than 1,083 metres.

Diametres and Distances From The Sun
(Approximate scale 1:560 million)
2.5 cm = 1 in. 1m = 3.3 ft

Planets	Diameter	Object	Distance From the Sun
Sun	25 cm	Basketball	—
Mercury	1 mm	Small pinhead	11 m
Venus	2 mm	Big pinhead	20 m
Earth	2 mm	Big pinhead	27 m
Mars	1 mm	Small pinhead	42 m
Jupiter	2.5 cm	Big marble	143 m
Saturn	2 m	Medium marble	256 m
Uranus	1 cm	Small marble	526 m
Neptune	1 cm	Small marble	823 m
Pluto	0.5 mm	Small pinhead	1.083 m

Compare the sizes of the planets in relation to the Sun, which is hardly visible in the illustration. They are in order of their proximity to the Sun: Mercury [1], Venus [2], Earth [3], Mars [4], Jupiter [5], Saturn [6], Uranus [7], Neptune [8], Pluto [9].

Origins

Around 4.6 billion years ago what is now occupied by the solar system was filled with dust and gas that evidently came from a supernova that had exploded earlier. All this matter began to condense because of the force of gravity. In that way a dense core formed that pulled together most of the mass, and that is how the Sun was formed. The rest of the matter continued to form a sort of disk around this star. The collisions among the particles of dust and the small rocks also caused them to condense around certain points, thereby producing the masses that we refer to as planets.

Bode's Law

This astronomer discovered an interesting numerical relationship among the distances from the planets to the Sun. First there is a numerical series made up of zero, which represents Mercury, and three for Venus, and the remaining numbers that stand for the planets are double the preceding one. If we add four to each number and divide by ten, we get a new series in which one is the distance from the Earth to the Sun and each number coincides almost exactly with the distance of the respective planet from our star.

Mercury	Venus	Earth	Mars	Asteroids	Jupiter	Saturn	Uranus	Neptune	Pluto
0	3	6	12	24	48	96	192	384	768
0,4	0,7	1	1,6	2,8	5,2	10	19,6	38,8	77,2

The Sun

The heart of the Solar System, this red giant is at the centre of our Milky Way. Turn the pages and find out more about the Sun – its origin, its significance and more. The Sun is more than just a fiery ball that keeps us warm, and here you will be fascinated to learn that apart from rising in the east and setting down in the west, the Sun has other engagements with its planetary neighbours too.

The Sun, our nearest star

The Sun is the central star of the Solar System. In ancient times people believed that the Sun was relatively small and very near the Earth. Now we know it is much larger than people first thought. Its radius is about a hundred times larger than the Earth and it is 150 million kilometres from Earth, almost 400 times further than the Moon. The Sun is a star, that is, a huge ball of hot gas. Unlike all the other stars, the Sun is the only one near the Earth. Planets move around the Sun attracted by **gravitational force.**

Our Nearest Neighbour

The next nearest star, Proxima Centauri, is 266,000 times further away than the Sun. So we know more about the Sun than about any other star. Like most stars, the Sun's energy is created when part of its matter is changed into energy by **nuclear fusion.**

Creating Energy

In the reactions that take place inside the Sun, **hydrogen** gas is transformed into **helium.** The Sun loses 4 million tonnes of matter every second, but because it is so huge, this loss does not affect it. During its life, which will last about 10,000 million years, the Sun will lose less than 0.1% of its matter.

SUN FACTS
Distance to the Earth: 150 million kilometres (12,000 times the Earth's diameter).
Diameter: 1.39 milion kilometres (109 times that of the Earth)
Temperature: In the centre : 15 million°C
On the surface: 6,000°C
Period of rotation: approximately 27 days

Here you can see the order of the planets, starting nearest the Sun: Mercury, Venus, Earth, Mars, Jupiter, Saturn, Uranus, Neptune and Pluto. The distance between the Earth and the Sun provides the conditions necessary for life to develop.

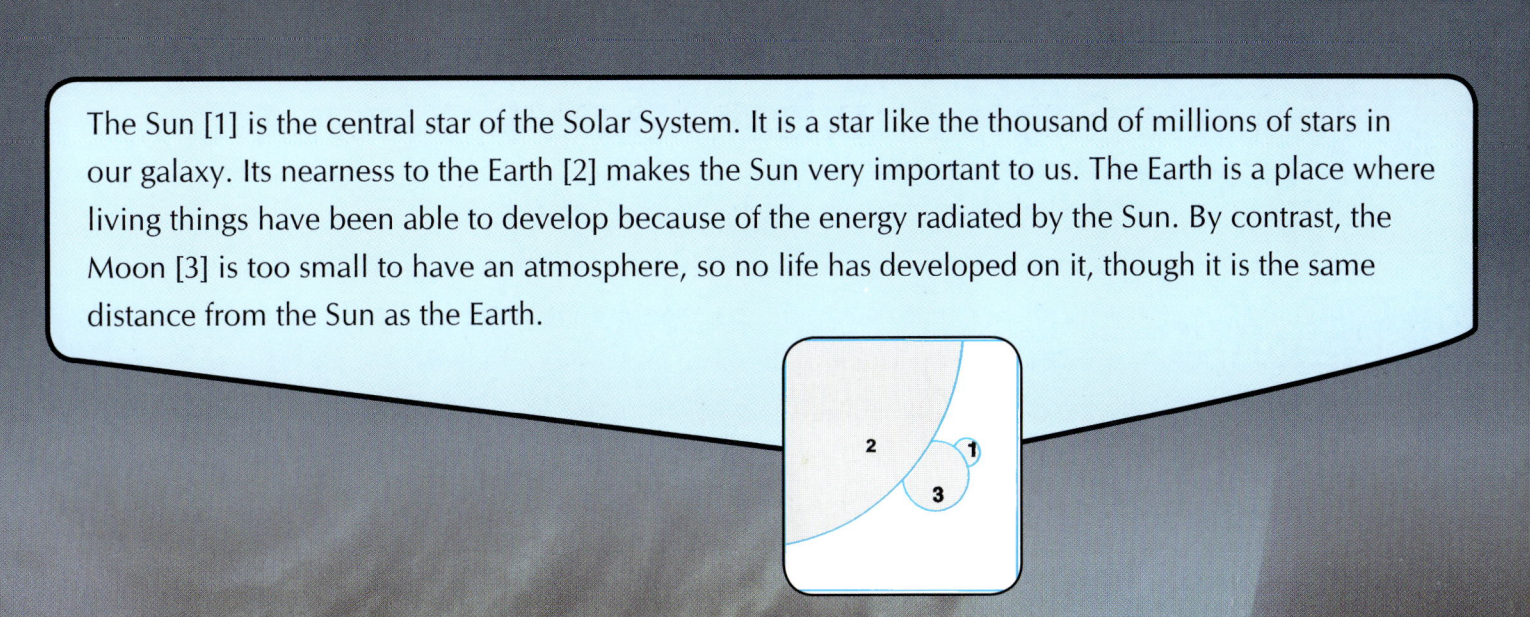

The Sun [1] is the central star of the Solar System. It is a star like the thousand of millions of stars in our galaxy. Its nearness to the Earth [2] makes the Sun very important to us. The Earth is a place where living things have been able to develop because of the energy radiated by the Sun. By contrast, the Moon [3] is too small to have an atmosphere, so no life has developed on it, though it is the same distance from the Sun as the Earth.

The Formation of the Solar System

Everything in the Solar System has the same origin: the Sun, the planets, their **satellites,** and the rest of mater that forms the **asteroids,** the comets, the **meteoroids**, and the inter-planetary dust. The Sun, like the rest of the stars, was formed from interstellar matter. This is gas and dust which form clouds among the stars of our galaxy.

A Chain of Events

About 5,000 million years ago, a cloud of interstellar matter condensed as it was going through a spiral arm in our galaxy. This started a chain of events in which the cloud started collapsing on itself because of its own mass. The central part, which condensed because of the mass of the whole cloud, grew extremely hot. The rest of the cloud flattened and began to rotate. It formed a thin disc which moved around the very hot centre.

The Sun Starts to Shine

When the temperature at the centre reached several million degrees celsius, the nuclear fusion of hydrogen began and the Sun started shining intensely.

The newly-formed planets were bombarded by meteorites. These are fragments of meteoroids.

The Solar System (outlined by the square) is near the outer edge of our galaxy, the Milky Way. The middle is made up mainly of hydrogen. It also has small amounts of other chemical elements.

The interstellar dust and gas that formed our Solar System gradually fell towards the centre where the Sun was formed [1]. The rest of the matter began forming a disc [2], in which clusters developed and began to collide, forming primitive planets [3]. These grew and formed the planets we see today [4]. Their gravitational force attracted more matter from the nebula which fell on them in the form of constant meteor showers.

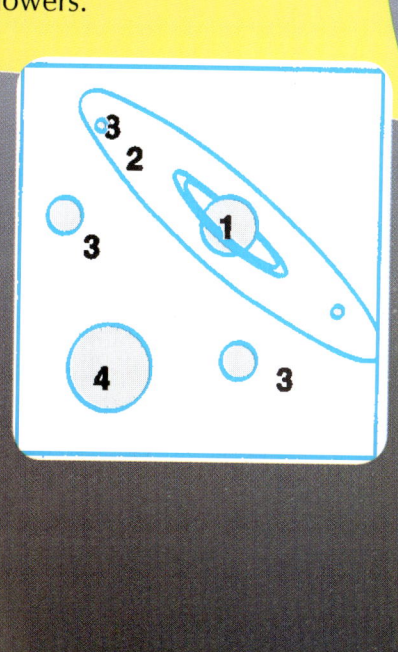

The Inner Structure of the Sun

The Sun, like most of the stars, consists of a series of concentric layers of gas. The visible surface of the Sun is called the **photosphere** (sphere of light). It is not a solid surface, but a layer of very thin gas.

Producing Energy

The nuclear reactions that produce the Sun's energy take place in its nucleus. This is the extremely dense and hot central part of the Sun. The matter in the nucleus is so hot that it can support the whole mass of the star without being compressed.

The energy is produced in the nucleus as **photons.** These are high energy particles of light. Those photons are absorbed and emitted by the Sun's **atoms** many times as they make their way towards the surface. They gradually lose energy and, at the same time, they make the matter in the outer layers of the Sun even hotter.

Layers and Temperatures

The temperature of the matter near the surface of the Sun is very different from that in the deeper layers. The difference in temperature makes the matter move in a saucepan. This is called **convection.**

Over the solar photosphere, there is a layer called the **chromosphere** (sphere of colour), only visible during a total solar eclipse. Further out from the Sun, the chromosphere turns into the solar **corona,** a very hot area.

During a total solar eclipse, the solar corona is visible. It extends a great distance from the Sun.

The layers of the Sun under the photosphere are not very good heat conductors. Convection movements are produced during which the gas below grows hot, rises, cools, and falls down again.

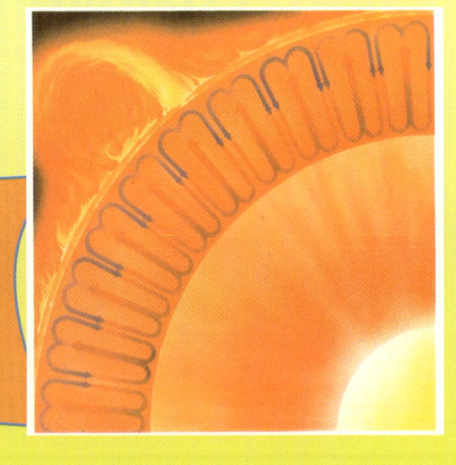

The central nucleus of the Sun [1], where the nuclear reactions that produce solar energy take place, takes up to a quarter of the Sun's radius. Inside the Sun [2], the energy is transported towards the surface. Near the surface, convection movements [3] like those in a pan of boiling water, take place. Sunshine comes from the surface or photosphere [4]. Sometimes we can see large arches above the surface called solar prominences [5].

Sunlight

Sunlight is white. In fact, it is made up of light of many different colours. The **spectrum** of colours that make up sunlight can be seen when a rainbow forms after a shower of rain.

Ultraviolet Light

When you look at a ray of sunlight through a **prism**, you see a range of colours from red through to violet. Each colour has a different wavelength. Visible light is one form of **electromagnetic radiation.** Beyond the violet end of the spectrum is a form of radiation called ultraviolet, with a shorter wavelength than visible light. This is invisible, but is responsible for tanning our skins during the summer.

Infrared Light

Beyond the red end of the visible spectrum is another form of electromagnetic radiation, called infrared. This too is invisible, but we can feel it as heat. It is given out by electric cookers.

Different Forms of Energy

Much of the energy the Sun gives out is in the form of visible light. But it also gives out ultraviolet, infrared and two other forms of radiation, radio waves and X rays. If our eyes could see these other forms of electromagnetic radiation, the Sun would appear very different. Using a camera sensitive to other forms of electromagnetic radiation, the Sun does not appear as a round disc. Some parts of the Sun give off more X rays than others, so the Sun does not appear uniform.

A rainbow appears when raindrops split up white sunlight into the spectrum colours: red, orange, yellow, green, blue, indigo and violet.

Spectrum of electromagnetic radiation

The Sun emits radiation in all the wavelengths of the electromagnetic spectrum. The appearance of the Sun in X rays is very different from the Sun in visible light. On the surface of the Sun, there are very bright areas that give off intense X rays [1] and dark areas that do not give off X rays [2]. X rays from the Sun do not reach the Earth's surface because they are absorbed by the Earth's atmosphere.

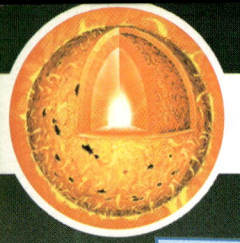

Observing the Sun

How can we find out what the centre of the Sun is like?

The **nuclear reactions** near the centre of the Sun generate huge amounts of energy. Most of this energy transfers to the surface of the Sun, where much of it becomes electromagnetic radiation, such as visible light. During the nuclear reactions, some of the energy becomes particle called neutrinos. These are thought to have no mass, and to travel at the speed of light. Neutrinos reach the surface of the Sun in a fraction of a second. From there, some of them reach Earth. Most of the neutrinos pass straight through the Earth.

Looking at Neutrinos

Special detectors have been built to detect solar neutrinos. These are huge tanks, buried in deep mines, so that no other radiation can get to them. The tanks contain a liquid that can detect neutrinos. Most neutrinos pass straight through, but the liquid can capture a few of them.

Surprising Results

The information collected by the solar neutrino detectors is rather surprising. They have detected fewer neutrinos than scientists expected from their knowledge of the Sun. So although the Sun is the best known star, it still holds many surprises.

A solar neutrino detector is made up of a huge tank of liquid which can capture neutrinos. It is submerged in water and buried deep underground.

All kinds of telescopes are used to look at the Sun. Most of them are on the Earth's surface. When scientists want to look at radiation that does not pass through the Earth's atmosphere, they have to send telescopes into space in rockets or in artificial satellites. The manned orbiting laboratory **Skylab**, shown in the illustration, had a solar telescope from which many observations of the Sun were made. Skylab was launched in May 1973, and remained in orbit until July 1979, when it entered the Earth's atmosphere and burned up over Australia.

Sun Spots

When we project the image of the Sun on to a screen with a small telescope, we usually see the solar surface marked with dark spots. These sun spots can be seen with the naked eye when they are especially large. (Warning: Looking directly at the Sun is dangerous. It can cause serious and permanent damage to your eyes and loss of eyesight.) Sun spots are areas on the Sun's surface that look very dark by contrast with the rest of the photosphere. Sun spots make it easy to watch the Sun rotate. Every day a spot follows a path which is parallel to the solar equator. When a spot disappears on the west limb of the Sun, some days later, if it is intense enough, it appears again on the east limb. The rotation period of the Sun, seen from the Earth, lasts about 27 days.

Sun Spot Activity

The number of spots on the Sun's surface varies. Sun spot activity follows a cycle of approximately 11 years. At the maximum point of the cycle of solar activity there are many spots on the Sun's surface. The most recent maximum point was in 1989. By contrast, at the minimum point of the cycle there may be no spots for many days. Some of the maximums are very intense, but occasionally there are long periods when there are almost no sun spots at all. This type of minimum happened during the 70-year period between 1645 and 1717, when it greatly affected the weather across the whole world.

Sun spots are uneven. Even spot in this group has a darker central part and a shaded outer part, called the penumbra.

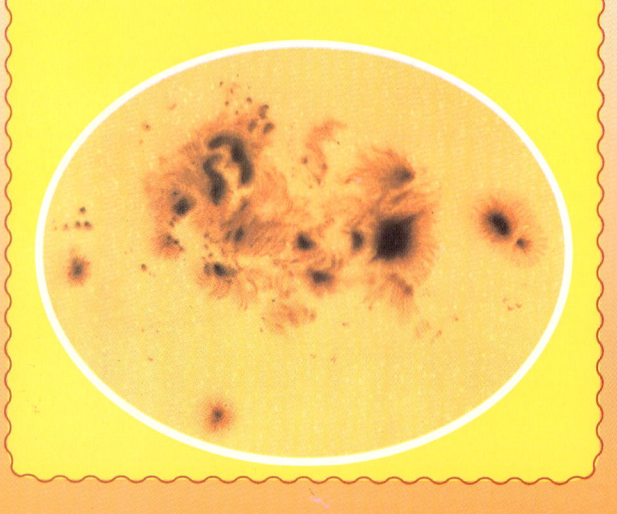

6 March

10 March

14 March

Sun spots appear to move from day to day as the sun rotates.

Sun spots are small dark spots on the Suns' surface. They are slightly colder and less bright than the rest of the solar surface. The normal temperature of the photosphere is about 6,000°C, but the temperature of a sun spot is about 1150° cooler. As it is cooler, the shine of a sun spot is much dimmer than the rest of the photosphere.

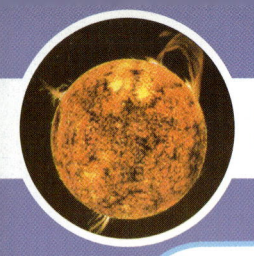

Solar Flares

Sometimes solar prominences or flares can be seen from the Earth. These look like large red flares that emerge from the Suns' surface and extend beyond the Moon's limb. This happens during a total solar eclipse, when the Moon completely hides the Sun.

Looking at Solar Flares

You can see solar flares without waiting for a solar eclipse. If you look at the Sun through a filter that lets in just the red light given off by hydrogen, you will easily see the flares. This is how scientists observe them. Solar flares are clouds of hydrogen that normally appears at the bottom of the solar corona and have a higher density than the rest of the corona matter. Flares on the Sun's edge are easier to see. They can also be seen on the solar disc, where they look like dark **filaments**.

Varying Shapes and Size

Some solar flares can be very large. The largest flares can reach thousands of kilometres in length. Some solar flares last for days or even weeks, while others come and go in a few hours. The varying shapes of solar flares are caused by the Sun's magnetic field which causes matter to move in snake-like tracks, curling or forming flaming filaments. The solar flares follow a cycle similar to the cycle of sun spots.

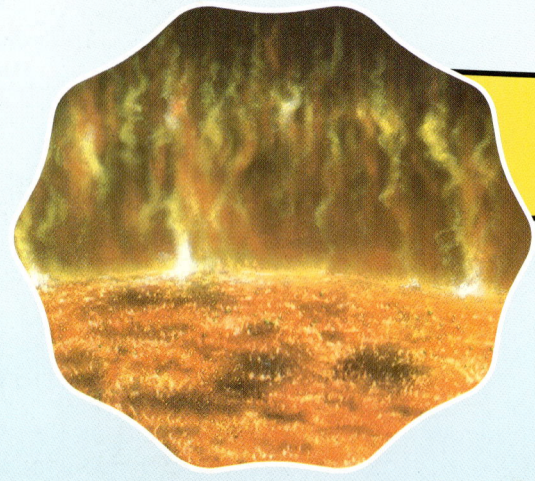

Solar flares often look like flames. The matter travels in wave-like paths caused by the Sun's magnetic field.

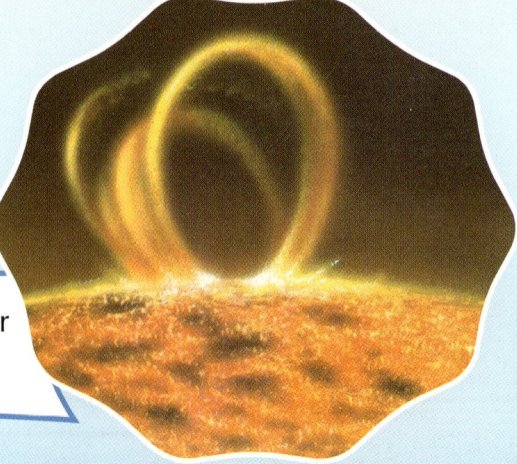

Looping solar flares are the most spectacular seen on the Sun.

Huge solar flares in the shape of arches [1] and flames [2] rise above the Sun's limb. Solar flares are formed by hydrogen that condenses from the soft solar corona. They fall on the Sun's surface following paths marked by the Sun's magnetic field. Solar flares use a large amount of solar energy and are the most spectacular phenomena that can be seen on the Sun's surface.

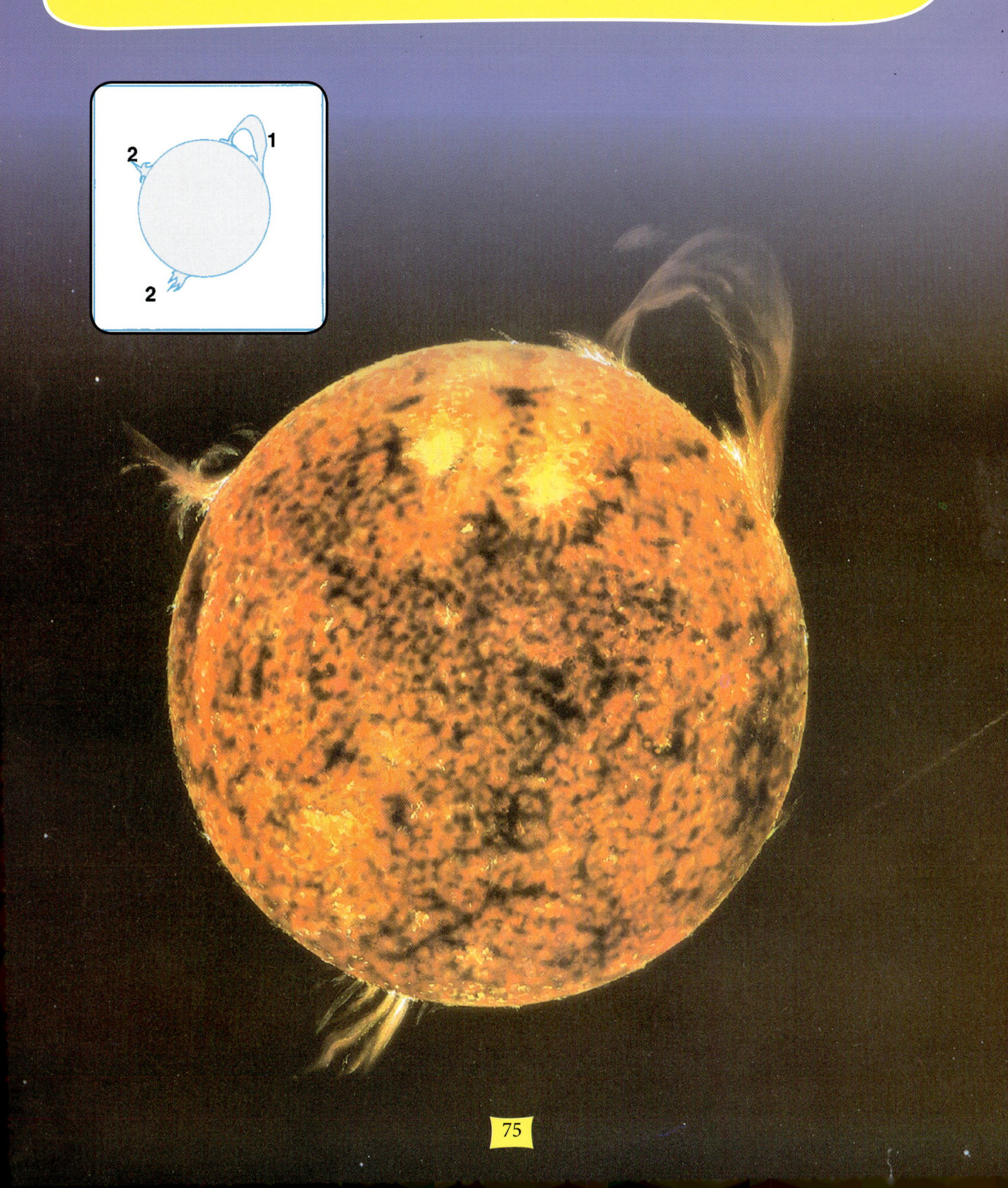

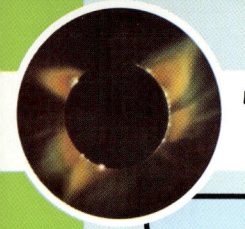

The solar corona

The Sun does not end abruptly at the photosphere. Above it, there is what we call solar atmosphere. At the bottom of this atmosphere, there is the chromosphere, which is a thin layer between the photosphere and the high atmosphere. The corona is the outer part of the solar atmosphere. It is a thin, hot area that extends a long way from the Sun. The best time to see the corona is during a total solar eclipse, when the Moon hides the solar photosphere. When this happens, the luminous halo that is the corona can be seen. Special telescopes are used to study the corona. Inside the telescope, a disc hides the sun's photosphere, as if an eclipse is taking place.

The Corona's Temperature

The temperature of the corona is extremely high: it can be more than two million degrees Celsius. At this temperature, matter gives off huge amounts of visible light, ultraviolet and X rays. However, the corona is so thin that it looks dim compared to the photosphere of the Sun itself. This is why it can only be seen well during an eclipse. The shape and extent of the corona also varies with the cycle of solar activity. During maximum solar activity the corona has long extensions that stretch out into space for great distances.

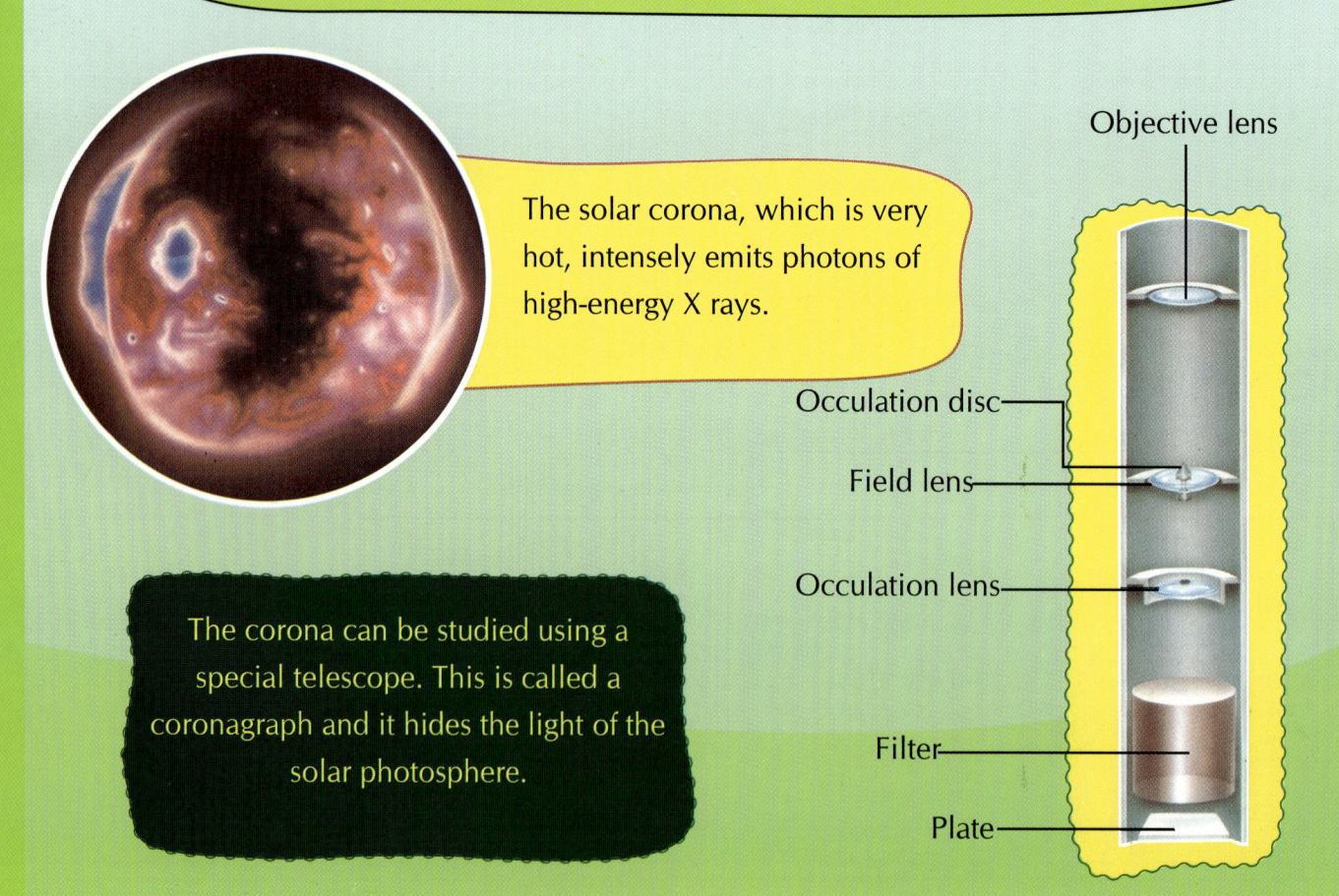

The solar corona, which is very hot, intensely emits photons of high-energy X rays.

The corona can be studied using a special telescope. This is called a coronagraph and it hides the light of the solar photosphere.

Objective lens
Occulation disc
Field lens
Occulation lens
Filter
Plate

During a total eclipse, when the Moon hides the light of the solar photosphere, the solar corona [1] appears in all its splendour. Then, it is visible to the naked eye. Several solar flares [2] can be seen near the solar limb. The shape and extent of the corona vary greatly during the 11-year cycle of solar activity. When it is most active, the corona can reach over distances larger than the diameter of the Sun.

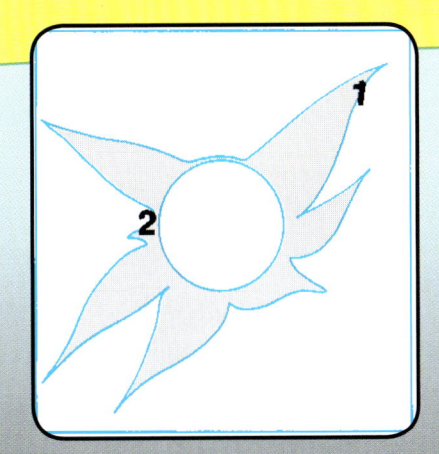

THE SOLAR WIND

The solar corona is the outer part of the solar atmosphere. It does not end abruptly in any precise place. Its temperature is so high that it is always throwing off matter in all directions. This matter—mostly a high energy plasma of hydrogen and helium—moves away from the Sun at high speed. This is called the solar wind. The solar wind is responsible for comets' beautiful tails. The solar wind is made up of free **electrons** and **hydrogen** and **helium atoms** (the main components of the Sun) that have lost their electron shell.

Incredible Speed

The speed of the solar wind is amazing: about 400 kilometres per second. Even at this speed, the particles which reach the Earth have travelled for about four or five days. So the Sun is continuously losing matter as it creates the solar wind. But the matter that forms the solar wind is very thin indeed. Near the Earth, the solar wind contains only about five particles in every cubic centimeter of space. This is far fewer than the best **vacuums** produced by laboratories here on Earth.

A Tiny Fraction

The amount of matter that the Sun loses in this way is approximately a million tonnes per second. But the Sun is so large that this is only a tiny fraction of its total mass, even if the solar wind goes on blowing with the same intensity for thousands of millions of years.

As the sun spins, the particles that form the solar wind move away in a spiral pattern.

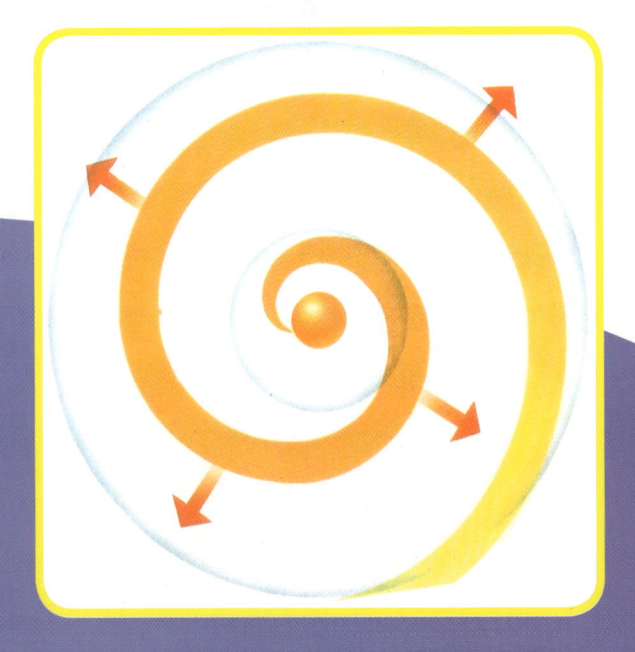

The solar wind is a diffuse stream of matter, given off by the Sun at a high speed. Comets are affected by it. The gas and dust that evaporate from a comet because of the Sun's heat are pushed by the solar wind, creating the spectacular tail of the comet [1]. Driven by the solar wind, the gas tail always points away from the Sun [2], no matter which direction the comet is moving in [3].

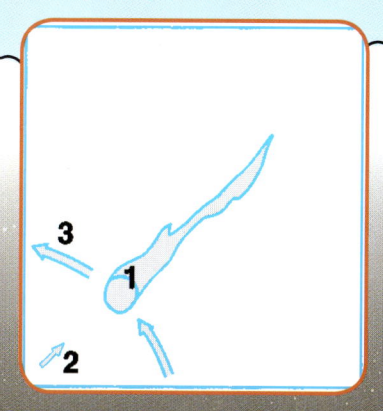

Solar eclipses

The Moon moves in orbit around the Earth, passing between the Sun and Earth every month during the phase of the new Moon. Usually, as we see it from the Earth, the Moon passes above or below the Sun. But sometimes the Moon passes exactly in front of the Sun, causing a solar eclipse. This usually happens two to four times every year. During a solar eclipse, the sunlight over a small area of the Earth is hidden by the Moon. For a short time, just minutes, night falls and the stars can be seen in the sky. Around the area where the total solar eclipse takes place, there is a large area where the Moon partially hides the Sun: when this happens there is a partial solar eclipse.

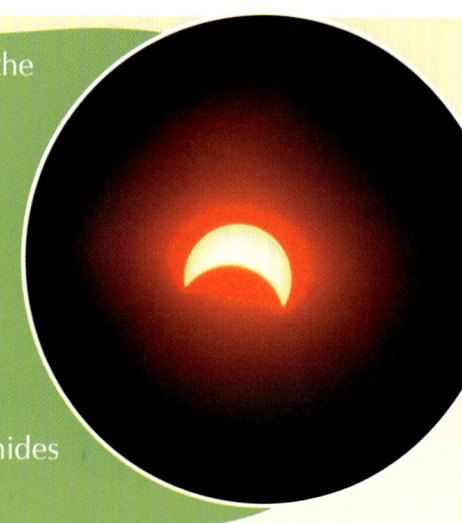

Size Differences

The Moon and the Sun, as we see them from the Earth, both seem to be the same size. Actually, the Sun is about 400 times larger than the Moon, but it is also 400 times further away. These differences in size and distance are what make the sun and the Moon appear the same size from the Earth. During an eclipse of the Sun, the Moon hides the solar photosphere as it is between the Earth and the Sun. When the intense light of the photosphere is hidden, the outer and much dimmer areas of the Sun become visible.

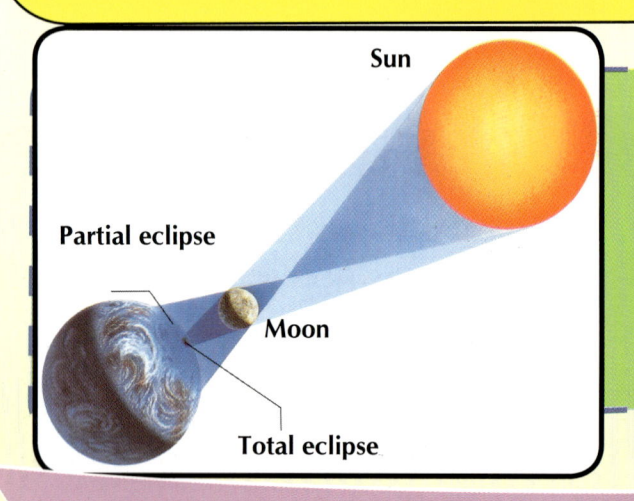

The moon completely hides the Sun in just a very small area of the Earth. Partial eclipses affect a much larger area.

TOTAL SOLAR ECLIPSES 1994-2000

Date	Areas where visible
23-4 October 1995	Somalia, Arabian Peninsula, Asia, Japan, Oceania, Australia
8 March 1997	East Asia, The Philippines, Japan, North-west of North America, Alaska
26 February 1998	Hawaii, Southern and Eastern North America, Central America, Northern South America, Caribbean Sea
11 August 1999	North-east North America, Greenland, Arctic Circle, Asia, Iceland, Europe, Northern Africa, Arabian Peninsula.

The Moon and the Sun, when seen from the Earth, appear to be the same size. When the Moon is exactly between the Earth and the Sun, there is a total solar eclipse. At the central point of the eclipse, the Moon hides the light of the solar photosphere and you can see the soft light of the solar corona. In the smaller pictures, you can see the different phases of the eclipse.

The Sun's influence on the Earth

The sun provides the light and heat needed for living things to survive on the Earth. It also has other influences on our planet. Ultraviolet radiation from the Sun reaches the higher altitudes of the Earth's atmosphere, about 100 kilometres from the Earth's surface. This radiation has created a layer in the upper atmosphere called the **ionosphere**. This layer reflects long-wave radio signals and allows radio communication over large distances between different continents on Earth. Most of the Sun's ultraviolet radiation is absorbed in the ozone layer, between 15 and 50 kilometres above the Earth.

Magnetic Fields

The Earth is surrounded by a continuous stream of particles blown from the Sun. These particles in the solar wind affect the Earth's magnetic field. The magnetic field of the Earth is called the **magnetosphere** and it extends into inter-planetary space. Iron fillings on a sheet of paper placed over a magnet will form straight lines with the lines of magnetic force, from one pole to the other. The particles that form the solar wind are affected by the Earth's magnetosphere, in a similar way to iron fillings around a magnet. Many of the particles are trapped in two regions around the Earth, called the **Van Allen belts.**

Approximately along the Earth's axis, there seems to be the equivalent of a large magnetic bar. The north magnetic pole of this bar is near the geographic North Pole.

In the ionosphere, a longwave radio signal can be broadcast from Africa, bounce back to the ground and be received in North America.

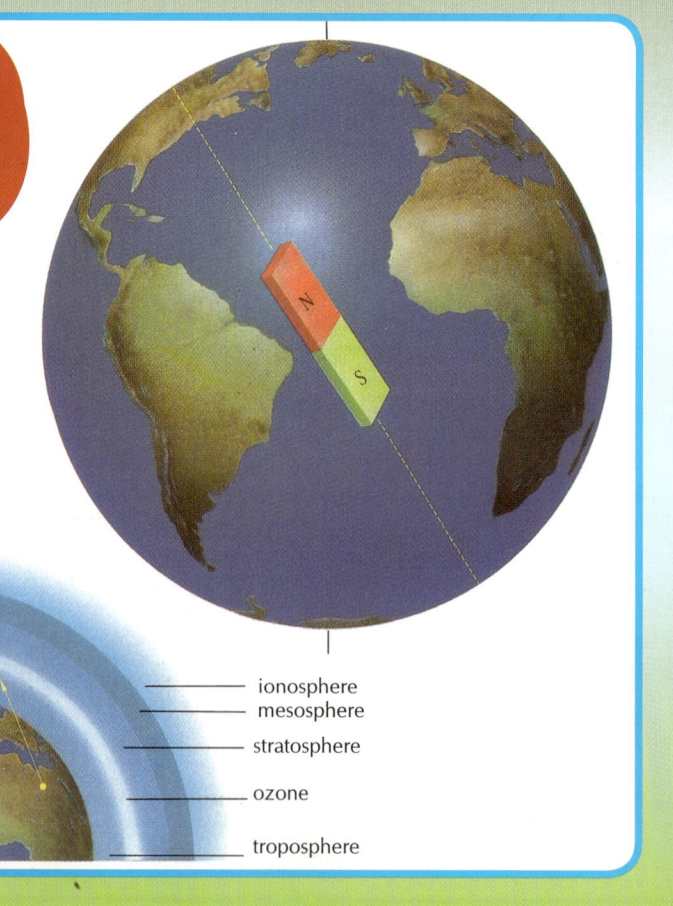

- ionosphere
- mesosphere
- stratosphere
- ozone
- troposphere

The magnetic field of the Earth extends into inter-planetary space, forming the Earth's magnetosphere [1]. The Earth is surrounded by two areas called the Van Allen belts [2]. These contain the charged particles from the Sun [3] that are caught by the Earth's magnetic field. The Van Allen belts were discovered by the first artificial satellites launched from the Earth.

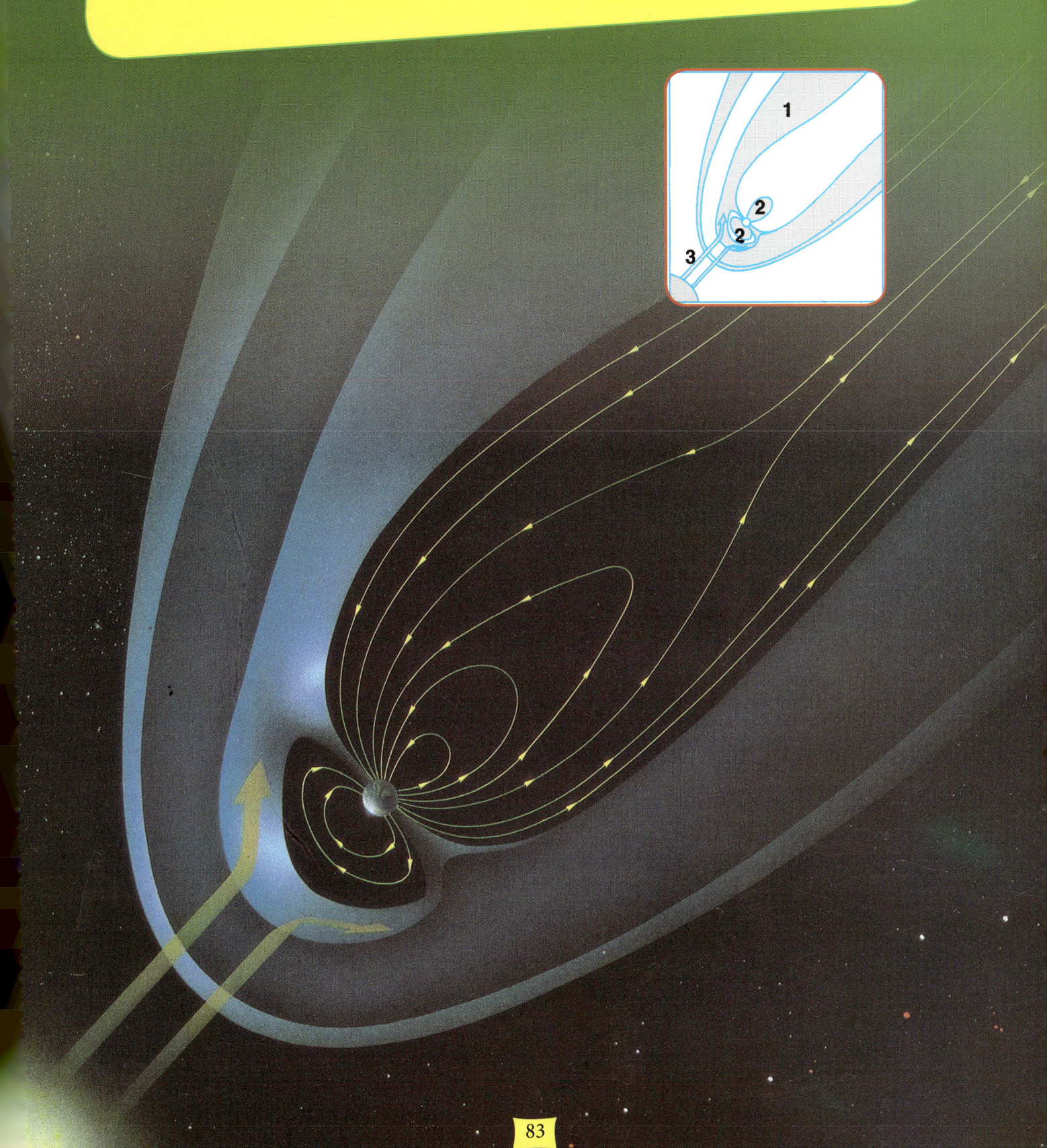

The Auroras

One of the most fascinating sights you can see in the night sky in high latitude areas are auroras. They are brilliant red, green or yellow lights which appear at night near the polar circles. The auroras are shaped like an undulating curtain, a flare, or sometimes an arch. They usually cover a great deal of the sky. In northern areas they are also known as the northern lights.

High Energy Particles

An aurora is caused by high energy particles given off by the Sun as the solar wind. Many of these particles are captured in the Earth's Van Allen belts. If a very large number of particles reaches the Earth, they can pass beyond the Van Allen belts. The particles travel along the lines of the Earth's magnetic field, and enter the Earth's atmosphere at the poles. The charged particles hit atoms of oxygen and nitrogen in the atmosphere about 100 kilometres above the Earth. This separates some of the electrons from the atoms.

Green and Red Wavelengths

When they are reunited with the lost electrons, the atoms give off green and red light. Auroras can appear near both poles. An aurora near the north pole is called aurora borealis. Near the south pole, an aurora is known as aurora australis, or the southern lights.

An aurora lighting up the night sky in high latitude areas is a fascinating and beautiful show. The atoms and molecules of the atmosphere produce the coloured lights of the auroras. Auroras are seen more frequently when there is a maximum number of sun spots. Sometimes they can be seen at latitudes of 40° or lower, though they usually appear closer to the poles.

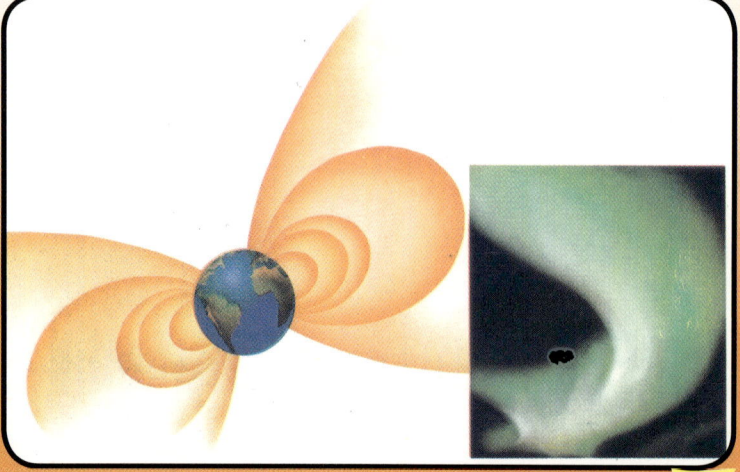

Auroras are produced by high energy particles given off by the Sun. They reach the Earth's atmosphere and travel along the lines of force of the Earth's magnetic field.

ACTIVITY: THE COLOURS OF LIGHT

Violet
Indigo
Blue
Green
Yellow
Orange
Red

You may obtain a spectrum with a non-flat piece of glass, but a prism will produce a better, brighter spectrum in which the colours are better separated.

Nature provides us naturally with the spectrum of sunlight. The rainbow that sometimes appears during a shower of rain shows all the colours of sunlight. On the inner side of the rainbow, there is the colour violet, and going outwards we can see the colours blue, green, yellow, orange, and red.

Make Your Own Rainbow

You don't need to wait for a rainbow to appear naturally. You can make one yourself using a garden hose. Put your back to the Sun and spray water into the air. A rainbow will appear in front of you, caused by the drops of water. If you want to study the colours of the spectrum of light more closely, you can make a rainbow appear indoors. To do this you will need a glass prism, a white sheet of paper and a room which has blinds or heavy curtains on the windows. You can use any non-flat piece of glass if you don't have a prism.

Rainbow Facts

- Rainbows are usually arcs of colour, but when seen from above they appear as complete circles.
- Most rainbows last only a few minutes, but some have been recorded as lasting up to 3 hours.
- Sometimes double rainbows form. In the second, fainter colours appear the opposite way round.

What to do

1. Pull down the blinds to darken the room.
2. Let a ray of sunlight in.
3. Catch the ray with the prism or piece of glass.
4. Reflect the rainbow that appears on the wall or on your white sheet or paper.

You will now be able to see the colours of sunlight in detail. Look at the range of colours and see how they change gradually from one end of the spectrum to the other.

It is easy to create a rainbow using a garden hose. Put your back to the Sun and spray water in front of you. A rainbow will appear.

THE MOON

There are a bundle of folktales and stories based around the Moon. This chapter gives you a ride to the brightest star in the sky. Right from the background to the time when men succeeded in inking their footprints in its bossom, the chapter provides all the information circling the Moon.

THE EARTH AND THE MOON

The Moon is our nearest neighbour in outer space. It is the **celestial body** closest to us, and it accompanies the Earth in its annual voyage around the Sun. The Moon is Earth's only natural **satellite**.

The Terrestrial Planets

Mercury, Venus, Earth and Mars are the four terrestrial planets. These are the planets closest to the Sun. They have very few satellites: Mercury and Venus have none; Earth, one; and Mars, two. But the Moon is an unusual satellite. It is much larger than the tiny satellites of Mars, and more like the larger satellites of the **giant planets**.

The Formation of the Moon

Scientists do not know exactly how the Moon was formed. At one time it was thought that the Earth once rotated much faster than it does now, and that the Moon was formed from material thrown off the Earth by this fast rotation. Most scientists now believe that the Moon was formed at the same time as the Earth from the same cloud or nebula of gas and dust that formed the Solar System, or from the remains of the material which first condensed to form the Earth. So, instead of considering the Moon to be the Earth's 'daughter' we should consider the earth and the moon to be 'sisters'.

The Moon is exceptionally large in proportion to the size of the Earth. Some of the other satellites in the Solar System are also large but are much smaller in comparison to their own planets.

Moon Facts

Distance from Earth: 3,84,000 kilometres
(30 times greater than Earth's diameter)
Time it takes to orbit Earth: 27.3 days
Diameter: 3,476 kilometres
(27% of Earth's diameter)
Surface area: 7% that of Earth
Volume: 2% that of Earth
Gravity: 17% of Earth's gravity

The Moon is Earth's only natural satellite. It is one of the largest satellites in the Solar System. Only four satellites (Io, Ganymede and Callisto of Jupiter, and Titan of Saturn) are slightly larger than the Moon. The Moon's diameter is more than a quarter of Earth's diameter. Only one planet in the Solar System can beat this. Pluto has a satellite called Charon, whose diameter is half that of Pluto. But Pluto is about the same size as our Moon, so Charon is much smaller than our Moon.

Exploration of the Moon

The Moon has been explored more than all the other celestial bodies put together. Exploration of the Moon began two years after the launch of *Sputnik 1* in 1957. This was the first artificial satellite of the Earth and the beginning of the space era.

The first **lunar probes** were launched to pass close to the Moon. This is what the Soviet probe *Luna 3* did. The American Ranger space probes were launched to crash against the Moon's surface.

A Soft Landing

The later space probes were of two types. Some spacecraft were designed to make a soft landing on the Moon's surface, such as the Soviet *Luna 9* and the American Surveyor probes. Other probes were sent into orbit around the Moon. This opened the way for direct exploration of the Moon.

Manned Spacecraft

The United States choose to send manned spacecraft to the Moon. Six **Apollo** spacecraft landed and their astronauts explored the area around the landing site. They collected lunar rock samples and left behind instruments which continued to function for years.

The Soviet Union choose to explore the moon using unmanned stations. Some of these collected lunar rock samples and returned to Earth. Others unloaded the **Lunokhod** exploration vehicles.

MAJOR SPACE PROBES TO SUCCESSFULLY LAND ON THE MOON

Name	Date	Landing area	Mission objective
Luna 9	1966	Ocean of Storms	Photographic exploration
Luna 13	1969	Ocean of Storms	Ground study
Apollo 11	1969	Sea of Tranquillity	1st manned mission
Apollo 12	1969	Ocean of Storms	2nd manned mission
Luna 17	1970	Sea of Showers	Lunokhod 1 vehicle
Apollo 14	1971	Region of Fra Mauro	3rd manned mission
Apollo 15	1971	Apennine Mountains	4th manned mission
Luna 20	1972	Sea of Fertility	Collecting samples
Apollo 16	1972	Region of Descartes	5th manned mission
Apollo 17	1972	Taurus-Littrow Region	6th manned mission
Luna 21	1973	Region of Lemmonier	Lunokhod 2 vehicle
Luna 24	1976	Sea of Crises	Collecting samples

The Moon has been explored by soft-landing automatic probes and by Lunokhod exploration vehicles, as well as by astronauts.

The Moon is the only celestial body to have been directly explored by human beings. Only 12 astronauts have walked on the Moon's surface. From 1969 to 1972 six Apollo missions reached the Moon, each carrying three astronauts. One person remained in orbit around the Moon while the other two landed to gather rock samples and carry out a series of experiments. On two of the Apollo missions, the astronauts drove a Lunar Roving Vehicle, pictured below. There have been no landings on the Moon by astronauts since 1972.

THE PHASES OF THE MOON

The Moon, like the other planets and satellites in our Solar System, does not give off any light of its own. The Moon shines in the night sky because it reflects sunlight. Half the Moon's surface, the hemisphere that faces the Sun, is lit up, while the other half is dark. The Moon travels around the Earth from west to east. The Moon's shape seems to change in a pattern that repeats every month. The different shapes of the Moon are called **lunar phases**.

The New Moon

The new Moon occurs when the lighted surface of the Moon faces away from us so we cannot see it. This happens when the Moon, on its orbit around the Earth, passes between the Earth and the Sun. The Moon is in its first quarter when it has travelled a quarter of its orbit around the Earth, a week after the new Moon. Another week later, we see the Moon completely lit up because it is now opposite the Sun. This is the full Moon. In the last quarter, another week later, we see only half of the Moon's disc.

The Moon's Cycle

When 29 1/2 days have passed since the last new Moon, the Moon again lines up with the Sun, ready to begin another cycle of its phases. This cycle is repeated just over 12 times during one year.

The Moon takes about a week to change phase and advance a quarter of its orbit around the Earth.

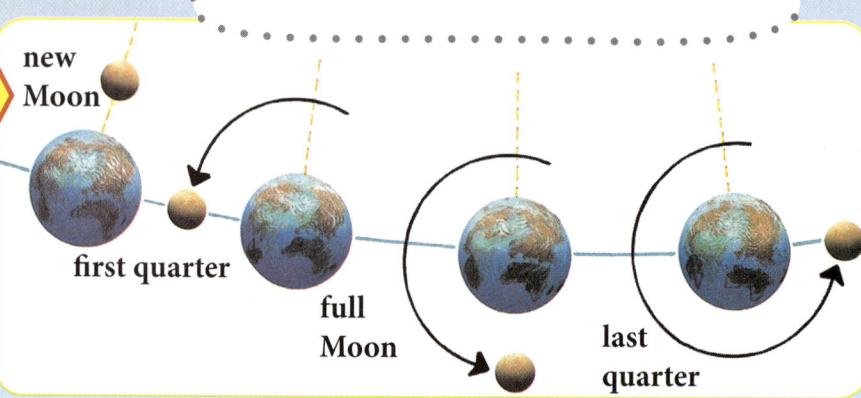

The crescent of the Moon is seen at dusk near the western horizon just after sunset. The lit-up face of the Moon is the part which faces the Sun.

A few days after the new Moon [1], the Moon appears in the sky in the shape of a thin wedge of melon. The Moon is now in its first quarter. It is seen in the west at dusk, setting on the horizon shortly after the sunsets. When the Moon is in its first quarter [2], we see half of the hemisphere facing us lit up by the Sun. During the full Moon [3], the Moon rises above the horizon just as the sunsets. During the last quarter [4], the Moon does not rise until late at night.

Eclipses

The Earth and Moon project long shadows in space, in the opposite direction from the Sun. These shadows are shaped like cones. When the Earth passes through the Moon's **shadow cone** an eclipse of the Sun, or **solar eclipse**, occurs on Earth. This is because the Moon passes in front of the Sun and hides it from our view.

Lunar Eclipses

In the same way, when the Moon passes through the Earth's shadow cone, the Moon is no longer lit up by the Sun, and on Earth we see an eclipse of the Moon, or **lunar eclipse.** Every year there are between two and seven eclipses of the Sun and the Moon.

Looking at Eclipses

There are about the same number of solar eclipses as lunar eclipses, but we can see the lunar eclipses from much larger areas of the Earth. By contrast, solar eclipses can only be seen from a very small area, under the Moon's shadow cone.

During an eclipse of the Moon, when the Moon enters Earth's shadow cone we can see how the Earth's shadow slowly covers the disc of the full Moon. During a partial lunar eclipse, only part of the Moon is in Earth's shadow. A total lunar eclipse can last over an hour.

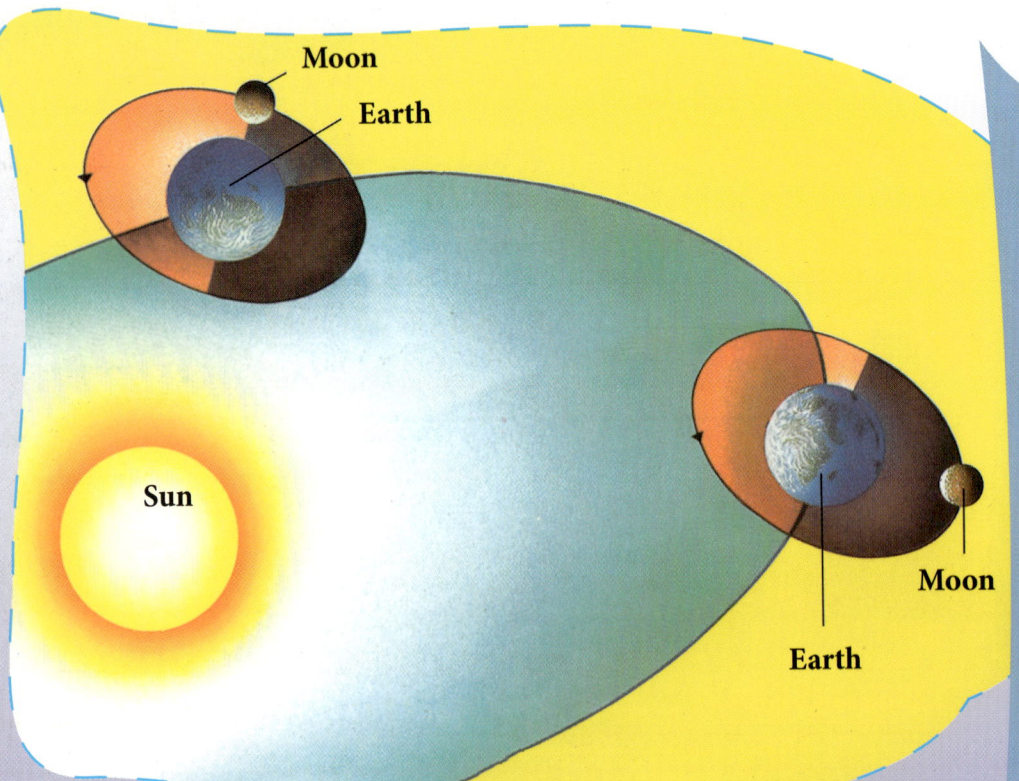

The Moon's orbit is tilted slightly to the plane of the Earth's orbit. If the two orbits were in the same plane, there would be a lunar eclipse every full Moon and a solar eclipse every new Moon. Most months the Moon passes above or below the Earth's shadow cone.

Lunar Eclipses from 1995 to 2000

Date	Type
15 Apr 1995	partial
3-4 Apr 1996	total
27 Sept 1996	total
24 Mar 1997	partial
16 Sept 1997	total
28 July 1999	partial
21 Jan 2000	total
16 July 2000	total

When a lunar eclipse occurs, the Moon enters into the Earth's shadow cone [1]. The Sun's light, which usually lights up the Moon, is blocked by Earth. The Earth's shadow starts to cover the eastern part of the Moon's disc [2]. When the Moon has completely entered the shadow cone, the total eclipse occurs [3]. At the end of the eclipse, the eastern edge of the Moon starts to come out of the shadow cone and is lit up once again [4].

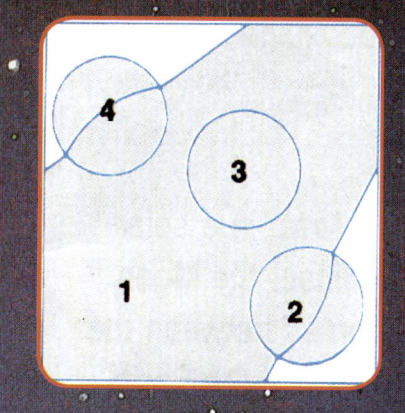

LOOKING AT AN ECLIPSE OF THE MOON

Lunar eclipses are quite frequent and are easy to look at. They can usually be seen from a particular place on Earth every year as long as clouds do not hide them from view. An eclipse of the Moon is a beautiful sight which can be seen by the naked eye (without using a telescope or binoculars). You can use binoculars, if you have a pair or can borrow some.

Earth's Shadow

When the Moon comes between the Sun and the Earth, the eastern edge of the lunar disc darkens. The eastern side of the Moon's disc is dark because it is that side which first moves into shadow.

When the Moon enters the Earth's shadow in the east, the Earth comes between the Sun and Moon and blocks out the sunlight reaching the Moon.

A Perfect Circle

As the Earth's shadow sweeps over the Moon, look at its shape. You will see that it forms a circle. This shows that the Earth is **spherical**, because the sphere is the only shape that makes a shadow which is always circular no matter which direction light shines from.

In a solar eclipse, the Moon comes between the Sun and the Earth. The Moon's shadow cone only covers a small part of the Earth's surface. From this area a total eclipse of the Sun can be observed. In an eclipse of the Moon, the Earth comes between the Sun and the Moon, and the Moon enters the Earth's shadow.

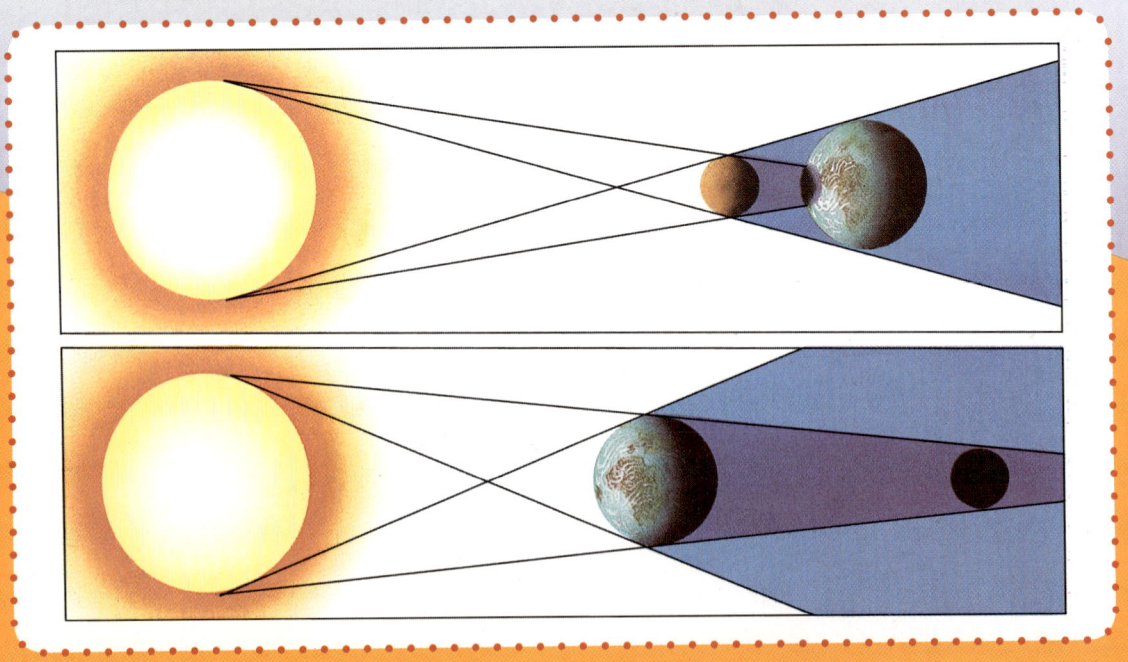

Moving Very Slowly

If you watch a lunar eclipse, try to imagine the Earth's shadow cone in space, and the Moon moving slowly into it. Although the Moon appears to be moving very slowly, it is actually travelling through space at more than 3,000 kilometres per hour.

In a lunar eclipse, the part of the Moon covered by the Earth's shadow [1] is not completely invisible. It is illuminated by a faint dark-red light. This reddish light fills the shadow projected by the Earth [2] into outer space. This colour is produced by sunlight passing through the Earth's atmosphere. The blue part of sunlight is scattered throughout the atmosphere, giving the sky its blue colour. Most of the red light gets through and reaches the Moon, giving it a reddish tinge.

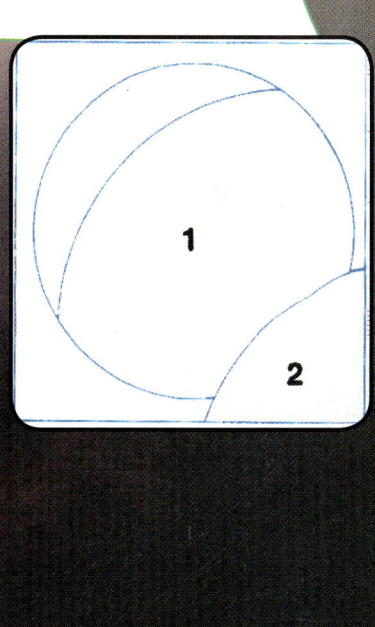

The Tides

Everyone who has ever been to the sea-side knows about tides. The level of the tide rises and falls twice every day. The rhythm of the tides affects the activities of people who work on or near the sea.

Changing Tides

For hundreds of years, people have known that the tides come about 50 minutes later every day, just as the Moon rises 50 minutes later every day. The force of the Moon's **gravitational pull** is part of what causes the tides.

The Moon's Influence

The influence of the Moon's gravitational pull is greater than the Sun's influence, because the Moon is much closer to the Earth. The size of the force that causes the tides — the tidal force — depends upon the difference between two points on the Earth. So a nearby object such as the Moon produces a greater tidal force than the distant Sun.

Water Bulges

Imagine the Earth is covered by a layer of water. The Moon will attract the water closest to it with a greater force than it exerts at the centre of the Earth. It pulls at the Earth's centre with greater force than it exerts on the water on the far side. This makes the water bulge out at two places in line with the Moon.

High and Low Tides

The bulges occur at two places on the Earth at any one time. At any one point on the Earth we will see two rises in the water level (**high tides**) and two times when the water falls (**low tides**) for each rotation of the Earth.

The Sun has much less influence on the tides than the Moon. But when the Sun is in line with the Moon, it reinforces the action of the Moon. This produces the highest high tides which we call spring tides. These occur during the full Moon and new Moon. When the Sun is not in line with the Moon in the first quarter and last quarter, high tides are lower and are called neap tides.

The succession of low tides (left) and high tides (right) occurs twice a day.

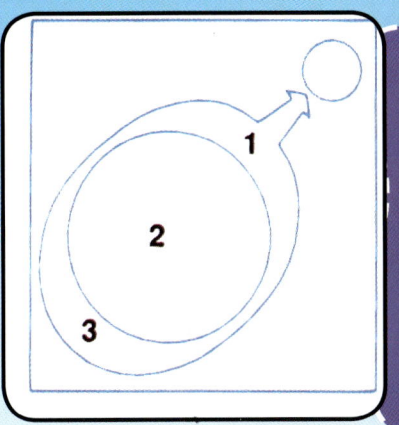

The Moon's gravitational attraction is stronger on the part of Earth facing the Moon [1] than it is at the centre of the Earth [2]. In turn, this force is more intense at the centre of the Earth than it is at the part of the Earth facing away from the Moon. This causes two bulges of water which form a straight line with the Moon. We see these bulges as the regular rising and falling of the tides.

Structure of the Moon

The Moon is made of a material which is lighter than that of Earth: its **density** is only 0.6 times that of Earth. This makes scientists think that the core or central part of the Moon which is made of heavy elements such as iron, is relatively small. It is about 1,000 kilometres in diameter. There is a rocky **mantle** around the core.

Lunar Quakes

The base of the mantle is where the small lunar quakes starts. These quakes occur regularly on the Moon. They have been discovered by **seismographs** left behind on the Moon's surface by Apollo astronauts. The information collected by these instruments shows that the Moon's interior is made up of molten material like the interior of the Earth.

The Moon's Crust

The top layer of the Moon is called the crust. It is about 60 kilometres thick and even thicker on the far side. The upper layer of the crust is made up of the remains of rock fragments of all sizes called **regolith**. This pulverized rock is the result of the bombardment of the Moon's surface by meteorites that has taken place since its formation. The regolith layer is normally between 5 and 10 metres deep but is a bit thinner in the area of the lunar maria. The pulverized rock layer that covers the entire surface of the Moon is what gives its dusty appearance. Scientists were afraid that this dust layer would swallow up any object placed on the Moon's surface. This idea was proved wrong when the first space probe landed. The probe did not sink. The Moon's surface was able to support its weight.

Lunar Rocks

The Apollo space missions and Luna automatic space probes brought back many samples of lunar rocks to Earth. These have been studied in detail. Scientists have found that they are basalt rocks more or less similar to some types of volcanic lava found on Earth.

The footprints of the astronauts sink into the dust to a depth of several centimetres. Since there is no erosion on the Moon, these footprints will always remain visible on the Moon's surface.

About 400 kg of lunar rocks have been analysed, such as those shown here. They were brought back by the Apollo and Luna missions. They are all volcanic rocks, such as basalt that we find here on Earth.

The Moon has a relatively small core [1], in which the heaviest materials, such as iron, are concentrated. Around the core, there is a molten rocky mantle [2]. The surface crust [3] is thicker on the far side of the Moon than on the side nearest to the Earth. This crust is covered by a regolith layer of dust and rock fragments of all sizes produced by the constant bombardment of the Moon by meteorites.

The Moon's visible side

The tidal force that the Moon produces on Earth tends to slow down the Earth's rotation and makes the day longer. In the same way, the Earth exerts a tidal force on the Moon, and this is much stronger.

A Lunar Day

The Moon takes the same time to rotate once on its axis as it does to orbit the Earth, so a day on the Moon takes one Earth month. This is why the same half of the Moon is always turned to Earth. This is not a coincidence. The force that causes tides in the Earth's oceans is also slowing the earth's rotation very gradually. Over millions of years, the Earth has exerted a similar force on the Moon, slowing its rotation to its current speed.

Lunar Seas

So from Earth we always see the same side of the Moon. When we look at it we can see some large dark spots. These dark regions are called lunar seas or maria because scientists first thought they were areas covered with water. We now know that they are actually covered with solidified volcanic lava.

The Terminator

The visible side of the Moon has a surface covered with craters except in the areas of the maria, which are much smoother. The craters are most easily seen in an area called the **terminator**. This is the thin area separating the light and shadowed sides.

The Moon spins on its axis, completing a rotation once every 27 days. At the same time it revolves around Earth completing one orbit in exactly the same time. This is why it always shows the same side to the Earth.

The Moon has two features on its surface which are most outstanding: large depressions filled with dark, solidified lava called seas; and large craters produced by the impact of falling meteorites on the Moon's surface.

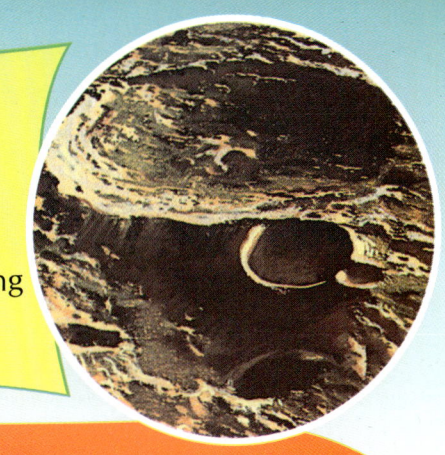

You can use a pair of binoculars to see the visible side of the Moon more closely. The large dark patches look like vast plains. These are the lunar seas. The large craters can also be seen easily and, if you use a map, you can find out which one is which and what each crater is called. Full Moon is not the best time to do this. At this time, the Sun's light strikes the Moon's surface head-on, and makes it difficult to see the relief of the moonscape. It is much better to observe the Moon in the first or last quarter phases.

Lunar maria

The lunar maria or seas cover a large part of the visible face of the Moon. These are regions that look darker than the rest of the Moon's surface. The lunar maria are relatively smooth, having few craters. So we know that the surface of the lunar seas is younger than the rest of the Moon's surface.

Volcanic Activity

The lunar maria were once large depressions in the surface of the Moon made by the impact of large meteorites shortly after the Moon was formed. The edges of these depressions form circular mountain ranges which surround the craters. About 3,000 million years ago, the Moon experienced a lot of volcanic activity. Lava flowed out of the volcanoes and filled the depressions, forming the lunar maria we see today.

Three More Seas

When the Moon is in the first quarter, another longish dark patch can be seen which is three different seas connected together: from north to south, these are the Sea of Serenity, the Sea of Tranquillity (where a human set foot on the Moon for the first time) and the Sea of Nectar. In the eastern hemisphere, which is visible when the Moon is full or in the last quarter, there is a group of large seas connected together. The largest is the Sea of Rains, which is surrounded by high mountain ranges. Some of the smaller maria are in the south. These include the Sea of Moisture and the Sea of Clouds.

Sea of Crises

Some of these seas are in the shape of a circle and are separate from the rest. One of these is the Sea of Crises, which is in the northern hemisphere of the moon near the western edge. This is the crater we see during the first quarter, a few days after the new Moon. Just under this sea we can see another dark patch which is the Sea of Fertility.

The lunar seas are large depressions filled with solidified lava. The depressions were formed when the Moon was young when large meteorites crashed onto its surface. Later, lava flowing from many volcanoes flooded the depressions, making a flat surface which later became scattered with craters.

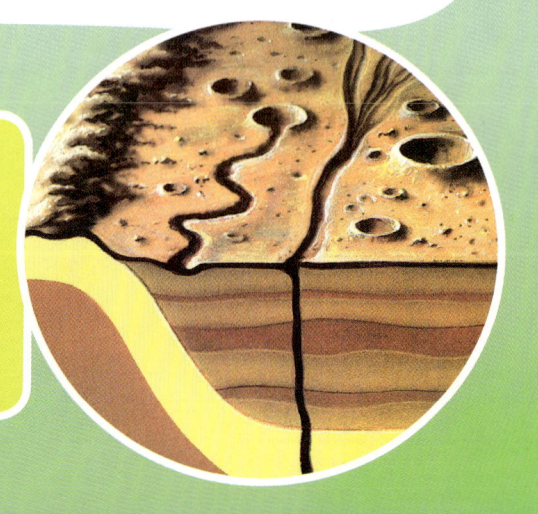

The Lunar Maria

Sea of Fertility (Mare Foecundatis), Sea of Serenity (Mare Serenitatis)
Sea of Tranquillity (Mare Tranquillitatis), Sea of Crises (Mare Crisium)
Sea of Showers (Mare Imbrium), Sea of Clouds (Mare Nubrium)
Sea of Moisture (Mare Humorium), Sea of Vapours (Mare Vaporum)
Sea of Cold (Mare Frigoris), Sea of Nectar (Mare Nectaris)
Ocean of Storms, (Oceanus Procellarum)

The Bay of Rainbows is located in the northern half of the visible side of the Moon. It is an old crater formed by the impact of a large meteorite about 4,000 million years ago. The depression later became partially filled by the volcanic lava that also produced the Sea of Rains. This area shows us the difference between a sea in the south which is flat and has only a few craters, and a mountainous region in the north which has sharp, craggy contours and lots of craters.

Lunar craters

Most of the Moon's surface is covered with craters. Craters are shaped like circles, have sunken bottoms and edges which are slightly higher than the rest of the Moon's surface. The walls of the edges are not steep but rise gently from the bottom of the crater.
Some craters have one or more peaks in their centres, and others have a smooth bottom. Often traces of debris from the impact and smaller secondary craters surround large craters.

Different Sizes

There are craters of all sizes on the Moon. The smallest are microscopic, while the largest are more easily visible and can be as wide as 100 or 200 kilometres.

Tycho

Tycho is a very large crater and has a diameter of 80 kilometres. It forms part of a mountainous zone in the south part of the moon below the Sea of Clouds. When Tycho is brightly illuminated by the Sun, during the full Moon, brilliant lines appear in the ground and shine out of the crater for a great distance. These lines are formed by material that was thrown out when the crater was formed.

The Origin of Craters

Most scientists now believe that the great majority of craters, like Tycho, were formed by the impact of meteorites crashing onto the Moon's surface. Some craters were formed by volcanic activity. We recognize these by their smooth lava-covered bottoms which have no peaks in the centre. One volcanic crater is Herodotus which is beside the impact crater known as Aristarchus.

The Largest Lunar Craters

- Alphonsus
- Aristarchus
- Aristotle
- Archimedes
- Clavius
- Copernicus
- Eudoxus
- Herodotus
- Hipparchus
- Kepler
- Plato
- Theophilus
- Tycho

A Meteorites crash into the Moon's surface. Unlike the Earth, the Moon has no atmosphere to protect it.

B The impact breaks up the meteorite and throws out material from the surface.

C As the material is sent flying in all directions, a round crater forms with a hollow depression in the centre.

D The edge of the crater forms a mountainous ring that rises above the surrounding surface.

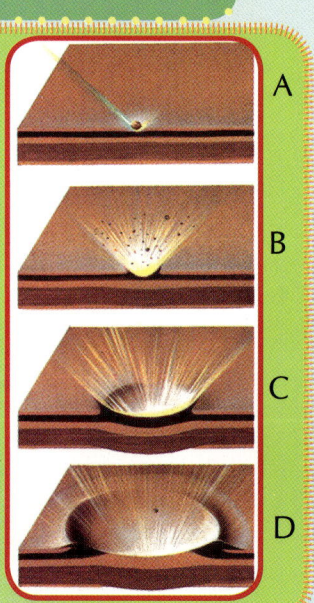

Copernicus, one of the Moon's largest craters, is over 90 kilometres wide. Found near the Ocean of Storms, Copernicus is a good example of craters created by the impact of falling meteorites. Its bottom is very irregular and has many mountain peaks [1]. This crater has sharply sloping walls [2] which rise as high as 5 kilometres above the bottom of the crater.

The Far Side of the Moon

The Moon takes the same time to spin on its axis as to orbit Earth. For this reason, one side of the Moon remains out of view from the Earth at all times. In fact, because we can look at the Moon from different places on Earth and since the Moon also wobbles slightly as it moves around the Earth, we can see a bit more than half of the Moon's surface. Over 40% of its surface still remains hidden when we look at the Moon from Earth.

The Far Side

In 1959, at the beginning of the space era, the Soviet space probe *Luna 3* managed to travel behind the Moon. The lunar probe sent back the first images of the **far side** of the Moon. These first photographs revealed that the far side of the Moon is similar to the side we can see, but there are some differences.

The Same Side

The differences between the two sides of the Moon tell us that the Moon has always shown the same side to Earth. The differences also tell us how the inside of the Moon is made up. Its crust, which is about 60 kilometres thick on the visible side, is much thicker on the hidden side.

Covered with Craters

The far side of the Moon is almost totally covered with craters, although they are not as large as those on the visible side of the Moon.
The largest seas are close to the edge of the visible side, and these can be seen, in part, from the Earth. One of the most important of these is the Eastern Sea, a large depression which is about 900 kilometres in diameter.

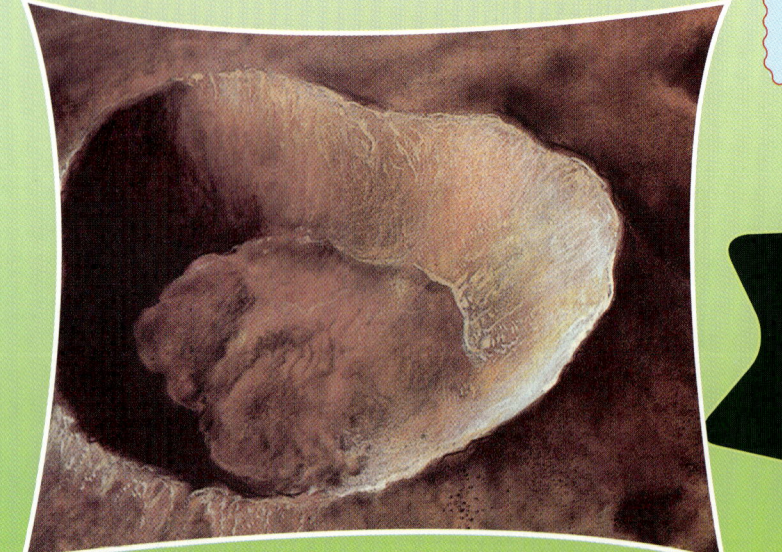

The Tsiolkovsky crater is one of the darkest on the Moon.

The Oriental Sea is a large depression, 900 kilometres in diameter, which is filled with dark lava and surrounded by rings of mountains.

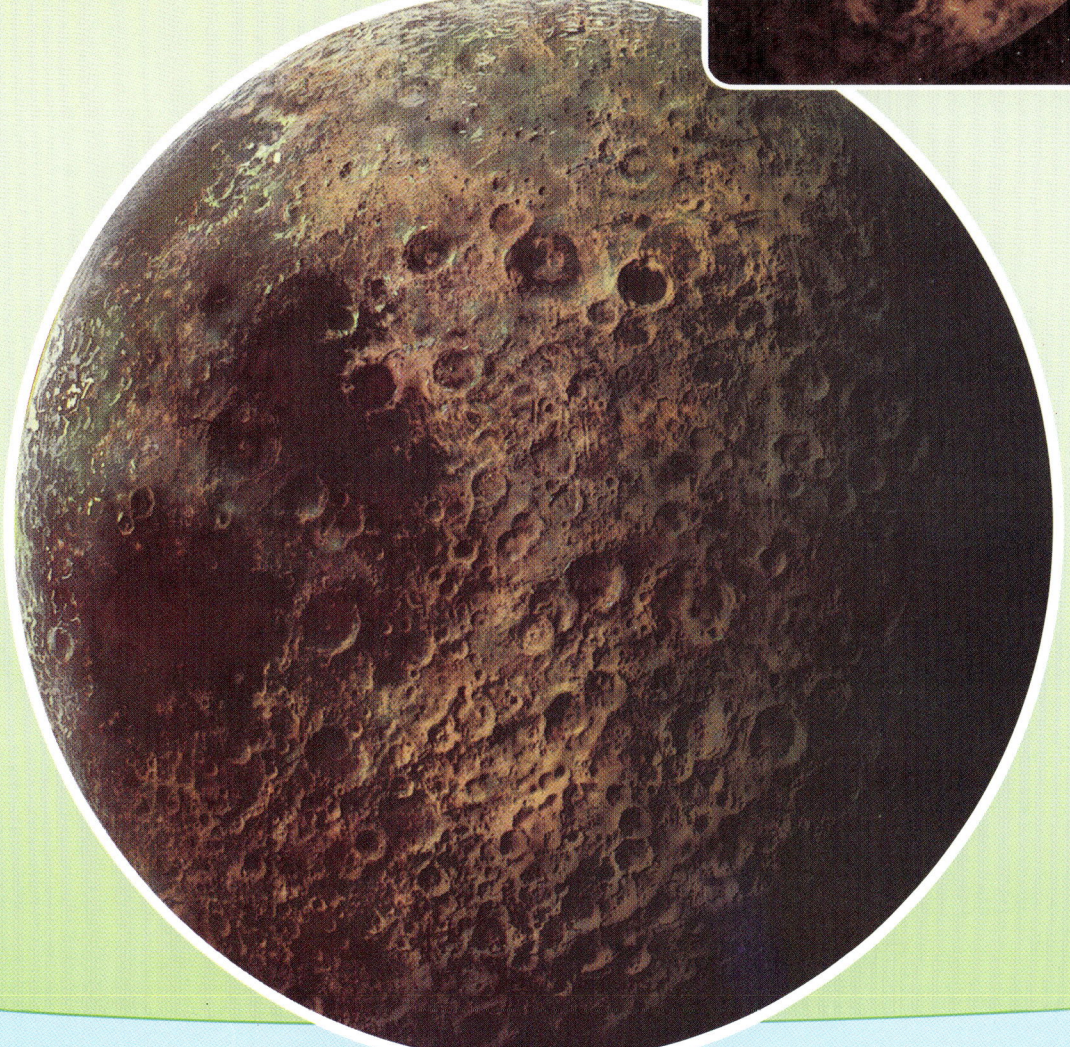

The far side of the Moon was a mystery until 1959 when the Luna 3 space probe photographed it for the first time. The hidden side is almost completely covered with craters, but has very few maria. One of the most important of these seas is the Eastern. Sea, whose mountains cover a large part of the Moon's surface. The Moscow Sea is one of the few maria which is completely within the far side. It is small, dark and circular, and it was first discovered by the Luna 3 images.

The Moon's Evolution

Even though the Moon is very close to the Earth, its surface looks completely different from the Earth's surface. The main reason for this is that the Moon is small and has a relatively weak force of gravitational attraction so it cannot retain an atmosphere like the atmosphere surrounding Earth.

Erosion

On Earth, there are no longer any traces of the ancient **craters** which were produced by the numerous **meteorites** that fell to Earth shortly after the planets of the Solar System formed. The craters have gradually been worn away by wind, rain, rivers and sea. This is erosion. Today, the Earth's atmosphere protects it from the small meteorites which fall towards it, burning up before they reach the Earth's surface.

Moon Craters

On the Moon, once craters are produced they remain unchanged unless another meteorite later falls in the same place. Many of the **depressions** produced by the impact of large meteorites when the Moon was still young became flooded by lava which flowed out of the many volcanoes that existed at that time.

The Oldest Regions

The numbers of craters found in different areas of the Moon tell us how old the surface is in that area. The longer an area has been bombarded by meteorites, the more craters there are on its surface. So the flat surfaces of the Moon, the **lunar maria**, are the youngest regions and have few craters. The oldest regions are completely covered by craters, many of which appear one on top of another.

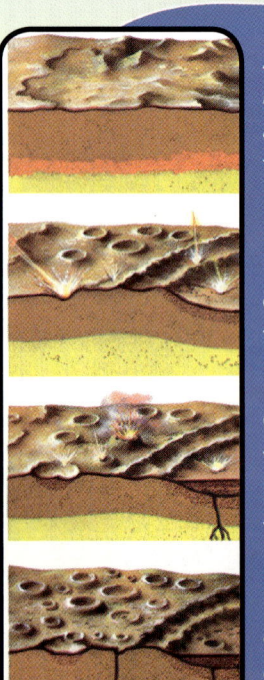

A The is how the surface of the Moon appeared 4,000 million years ago when the Moon had just been formed.

B Later the Moon's surface was changed by the constant showers of falling meteorites.

C About 3,000 million years ago, intense volcanic activity occurred. The lava thrown out by volcanoes flooded the ancient craters and formed the lunar maria.

D When the volcanic activity stopped, the appearance of the lunar surface was changed again by the impact of falling meteorites, which created new craters.

The Moon 4,000 million years ago [1], 3,000 million years ago [2], and now [3]

Activity: Earth and Moon models

We know that the Moon is more or less a quarter the size of the Earth and that it is about 30 times the Earth's diameter away from us. You don't need a powerful telescope or a trip in a spaceship to look at the Earth-Moon system. Instead you can make a model of the Earth and Moon yourself and look at the phases of the Moon and the eclipses in your own back garden or in the park.

You Will Need:
- 1 ball about 1cm in diameter
- 1 ball about 4cm in diameter
- a hammar and 2 long nails
- a wooden stick 120cm long

If you can't find balls of the right size you can make your own from plasticine — these will be just as good.

Making Your Earth-Moon Model

1. Take the hammer and hammer the two nails into the stick, one at each end. The nails need to be long enough to pierce the wood so that the points stick out about 1cm. Ask an adult for help if you need it.
2. Take the large ball and stick it onto the end of one of the nails on the stick.
3. Put the other ball on the nail at the other end of the stick.

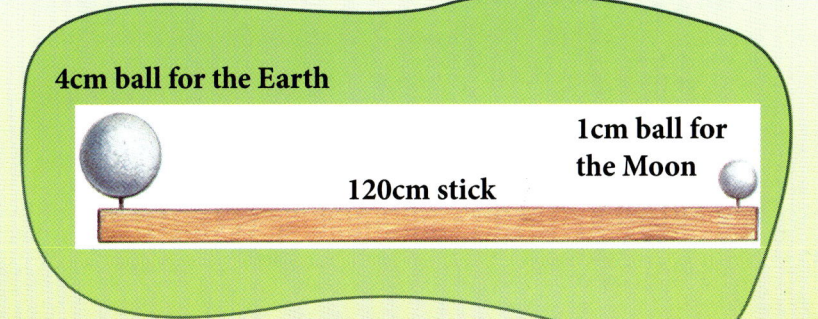

4cm ball for the Earth

1cm ball for the Moon

120cm stick

If you line up the Sun, the Earth-ball and the Moon-ball, the Moon-ball is left dark. This is an eclipse of the Moon.

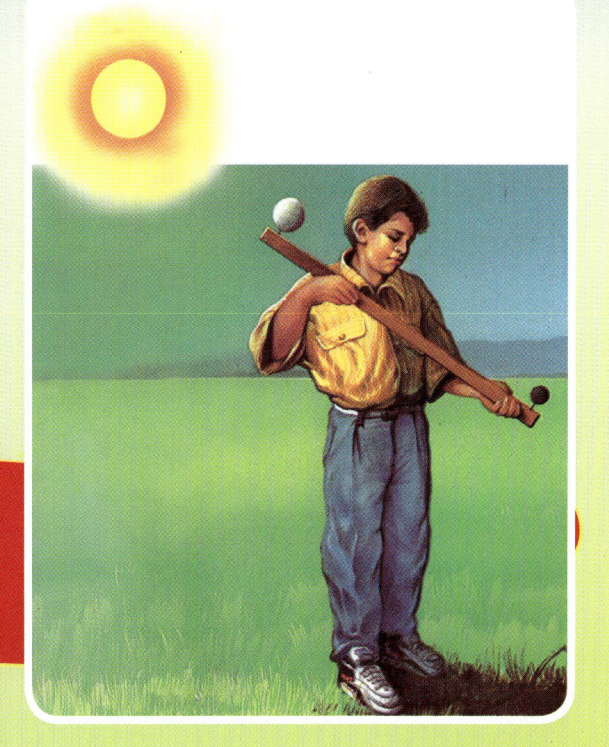

You should now have a model of the Earth-Moon system which you can use to look at the phases of the Moon and the eclipses.

What to Do

1. Choose a sunny day when you can see the Moon in the sky (in the morning if the Moon is in its last quarter, or in the afternoon if it is in its first quarter).
2. Take your Earth-Moon system model and find a place that is bright and sunny.
3. Now put the large ball which is Earth close to your eye and point the stick towards where you can see the real Moon in the sky.

You will see that the Moon-ball and the real Moon seem the same size. They are lit up by the Sun in the same way. You are now looking at a phase of the Moon.

4. Now stand with the Sun to one side and hold the stick in both hands with the Earth-ball pointing towards the Sun and the Moon-ball towards the ground.
5. Line up the stick with the Sun (you can use the stick's shadow on the ground to help you).
6. Now line up the Sun, the Earth-ball and the Moon-ball.

Warning: NEVER look directly at the Sun – it can damage your eyes and cause blindness.

You will see how the Earth blocks the Moon from the Sun. This is an eclipse of the Moon.

If you point the stick towards the Moon, you will see the Moon-ball lit up by the Sun in the same phase as the real Moon.

Stars

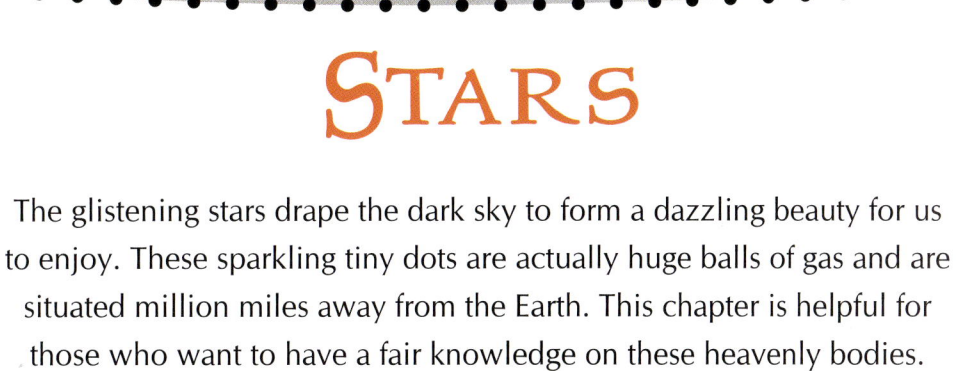

The glistening stars drape the dark sky to form a dazzling beauty for us to enjoy. These sparkling tiny dots are actually huge balls of gas and are situated million miles away from the Earth. This chapter is helpful for those who want to have a fair knowledge on these heavenly bodies.

The distance to the stars

At night the stars simply appear as points of light in the sky. There are all kinds; some are very bright and others are faint. The brightest are of magnitude designations that are less than zero. The faintest ones that can be seen with the naked eye are of magnitude six.
In our daily life, we can tell how far away the objects we see are because we have two eyes. Because our eyes are slightly separated, each one sees a slightly different image. Try stretching your arm out and looking at your raised thumb, first closing one eye, and then the other. You will see how the position of your thumb in relation to the back-ground appears differently to each eye. With the stars, we can do something similar. If we take advantage of the Earth's movement around the Sun and observe the stars six months apart, we can measure how the positions of the closest stars change slightly in relation to the ones that are farthest away. This change allows us to calculate their distances from the Earth. It turns out that the closest stars are so far away that their light takes about four years to reach us.

We say that they are about four **light years** away. Most of the stars we see at night are much further away, tens or hundreds of light years away. What would the Sun look like if it were as far away as other stars, for example, 30 light years away? It would be a fifth-magnitude star, barely visible in the sky to the naked eye. The only difference between the stars and the Sun is that we are much closer to the Sun so it looks brighter to us.

We can determine the distance to a closer star (A) by observing its apparent position relative to the most distant stars (B), and comparing it to its apparent position six months later. Earth's two positions (C) are 180 million miles (300 million kilometres) apart, twice the distance between Earth and the Sun (D). The different positions of the earth let us see a slight difference in the position of the nearby stars.

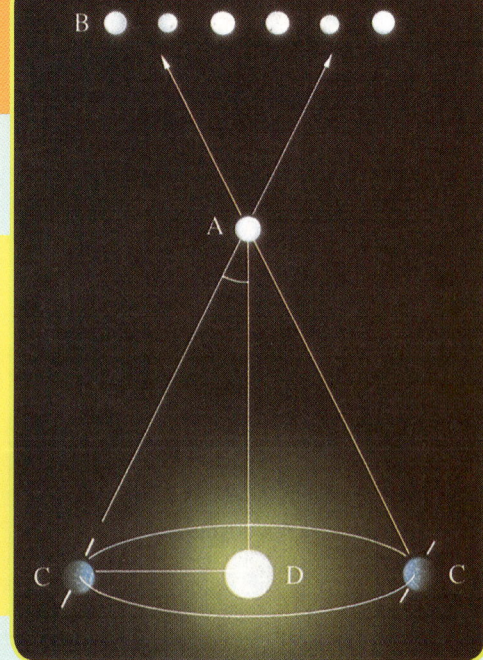

We see the stars in a constellation as being in the same area of the sky as if they are at the same distance. In reality, they are at a variety of distances, and very far away.

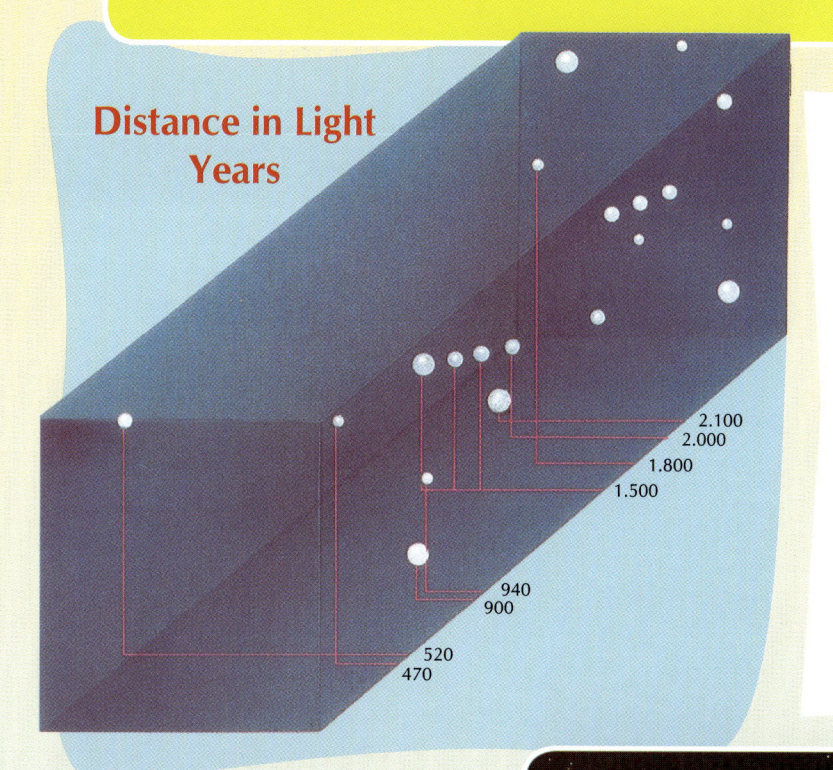

Distance in Light Years

2.100
2.000
1.800
1.500
940
900
520
470

Have you ever noticed the colour of the stars? The light they put out varies some-what in colour from one-star to another. In some cases you can see this difference easily. For example, in the constellation Orion, which is visible in the evening around December, the two brightest stars have distinct colours: Betelgeuse, in the northeast corner, emits a blue-white light. The stars have whole range of colours, from red to orange, yellow, white, and finally blue-white.

The Orion nebula is a luminous cloud of interstellar gas, illuminated by young stars inside it. New stars are being born now in that cloud. The great nebula in Orion can be seen with the naked eye in the constellation of the same name. It is one of the most beautiful in the sky. Four very bright stars represent the shoulders and knees of Orion, the mythological giant. Three bright stars in a line form Orion's belt. A sword hangs from his belt, and in the middle of it the Orion nebula can be seen as a somewhat blurry object.

WHY DO THE STARS SHINE?

The stars shine because they are hot. But where does a star get its energy to be hot? Until fairly recently, the answer to this question was unknown. It was Albert Einstein, developer of the theory of relativity at the beginning of this century, who answered this question: a small quantity of matter can be transformed into a large quantity of energy.

The stars are mostly made up of hydrogen. Hydrogen is the simplest natural element and the most common one in the universe. A hydrogen atom consists of a nucleus with a single proton and an electron. The matter at the centre of the star is very compressed by the weight of the star itself. This causes the protons that form the nuclei of the hydrogen atoms to collide violently with each other. As a result of these collisions, four hydrogen nuclei can come together to form a nucleus of helium. The helium nucleus is made up of two protons and two neutrons. During this process of **fusion**, two protons are transformed into neutrons, emitting a positron (a light particle like an electron, but with a positive charge). The helium nucleus weights slightly less than the four hydrogen nuclei that formed it. This small quantity of matter that has disappeared releases a large quantity of energy.

Like a star, a nuclear power station gets its energy from nuclear reactions. But instead of getting it from the fusion of light nuclei, the power station gets energy from fission—the splitting—of heavy nuclei.

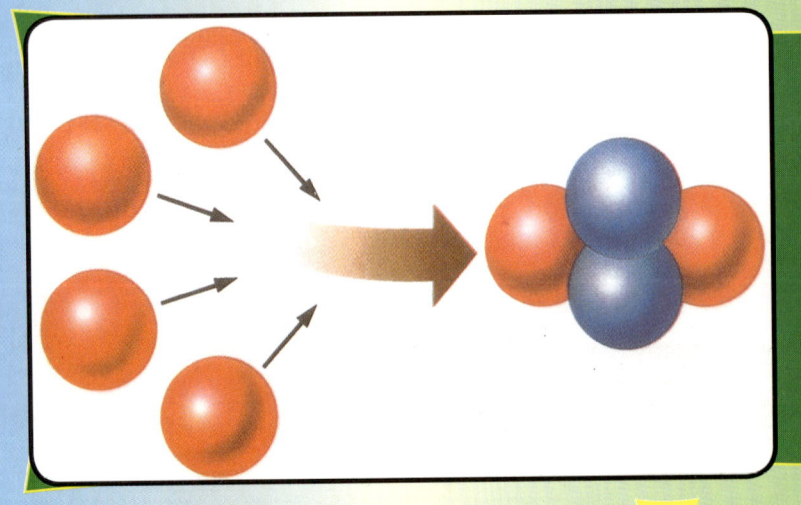

The nucleus of most stars is a true nuclear reactor, where fusion reactions take place. The hydrogen nuclei collide violently with each other. Four protons can merge and create a helium nucleus with two protons and two neutrons.

The supernova 1987A 1 suddenly appeared on February 24, 1987, in the Great Magellanic Cloud 2 in the southern hemisphere. In this galaxy, which is close to ours, an old star had burst in an immense explosion. What had before been an ordinary star was transformed in a matter of hours into the most brilliant one in that part of the sky. Some stars end their lives this way, with a huge supernova explosion. Other stars also die, but in less spectacular ways.

GROUPS OF STARS

The great majority of stars are not isolated, but rather form systems of two, or sometimes more, stars that are near each other in space. In these double systems, the stars revolve around each other because of the gravitational force between them. Milzar and Alcor, in Ursa Major, are a good example that can be seen with the naked eye.

Other groups of stars, called **star clusters,** contain hundreds or even thousands of stars. These are groups of stars that were formed simultaneously in the same part of the galaxy. One of the most beautiful star clusters is the one known as the Pleiades. Six stars that form a small dipper shape can be seen with the naked eye in the constellation Taurus. With some binoculars small groups of stars can be distinguished, and with a telescope hundreds of stars can be seen in the cluster. These stars are blue and luminous, all of the same age, and were formed recently from the same cloud of interstellar matter.

Some clusters that can be seen in the sky are extremely crowded. They have a spherical shape, and contain many, many stars. These are called **globular clusters**. There are many globular clusters near the constellation Sagittarius, which marks the centre of our galaxy.

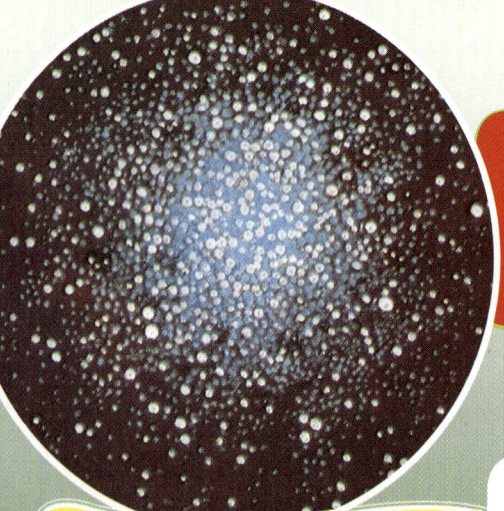

The globular cluster in the constellation Hercules is made up of more than a million stars crowded together. The stars in this cluster are among the oldest in our galaxy.

In Ursa Major, Mizar and Alcor (in the box) are visible with the naked eye. With a telescope, though, you can see (as shown in the enlarged box) that Mizar is a system made up of two stars.

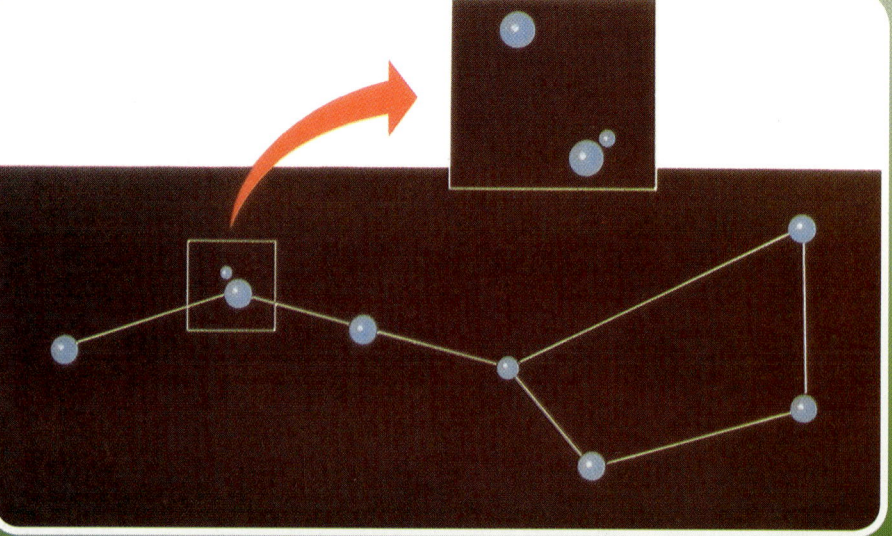

The Pleiades are a group of young blue stars in the constellation Taurus. The cluster is made up of hundreds of stars, the brightest of which can be seen with the naked eye. Each of these stars 1 is surrounded by a halo of gas and dust 2 left over from the intersteller matter from which they were formed. The cloudiness around these stars will disperse completely when the stars are older.

The birth of the stars

We know that stars must have been formed at some time in the past. What were they formed from? The only reasonable answer is from existing gas and dust among the stars in the galaxy. This is called **interstellar matter**. Under normal conditions, interstellar matter is not visible, but when illuminated by a hot, luminous star, it forms **bright nebulas** that have a rosy colour. The force governing this whole process of formation and, in fact, the star's subsequent life, is gravity. According to one theory, when a cloud of interstellar matter crosses a spiral arm of the galaxy, it begins to condense and the internal gravitational force increases. This makes the cloud contract more rapidly. As the matter condenses, it breaks into pieces and gets hotter. The centre of any very large piece reaches temperatures over a million degrees, giving rise to a **protostar**. Because of this high temperature, a reaction starts among the hydrogen nuclei.

When a cloud of interstellar matter contracts enough, a very hot protostar is formed in the middle of it.

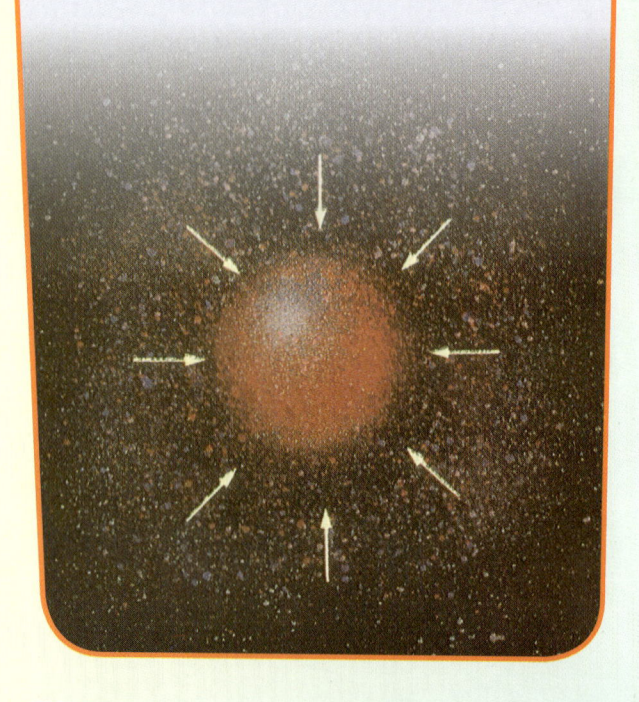

The Orion Nebula, an area where many stars are being formed, is in the lower half of the constellation Orion.

The energy produced at the centre of the protostar stops the contraction and a new star has been formed. The remnants of the initial cloud form a flat disc that revolves around the star. This matter can end up condensing and forming the planets that accompany the newly formed star.

Stars are formed by the gravitational contraction of a cloud of interstellar dust and gas. A dark nebula 1 composed of interstellar dust hides the stars behind it. The Horsehead Nebula 2 protrudes from this dark nebula behind a bright nebula 3. The brightest star 4 is Zeta Orionis, the star on the left in Orion's belt. The Horsehead nebula is a region in our galaxy where new stars are being formed even today.

How do stars die?

Many stars spend most of their old age as red giants. Their nuclei are made up of very hot and compressed helium. When the temperature in the centre of these stars reaches 200 million degrees, the helium nuclei begin to react. These new nuclear reactions bring about heavier elements of carbon, nitrogen, and oxygen. The energy produced by these reactions momentarily stops the contraction in the star. The wrapping of the star is so swollen that the star begins to lose its outer layers, releasing a hydrogen gas bubble. These bubbles are known as **planetary nebulas**, because when seen through a small telescope they appear in the shape of a disc, somewhat similar to a planet. One of the most spectacular examples of a planetary nebula is the Ring Nebula in the constellation Lyra. The gas bubble appears as a ring because only its edges are visible. In the centre of a planetary nebula there is always a blue-white star. This is the old nucleus of a very compressed and hot red giant which has become exposed after losing its wrapping. Such stars are called **white dwarfs**. They are made up of ice, carbon, and oxygen. They have approximately the same amount of matter as the Sun, but are only as big as the Earth. They have a very high density, thousands of times that of water. The Sun, and all other stars with similar masses, will end their lives as white dwarfs. They are inert stars that will not evolve further. They start to cool over a period of billions of years, until they become dark dwarfs.

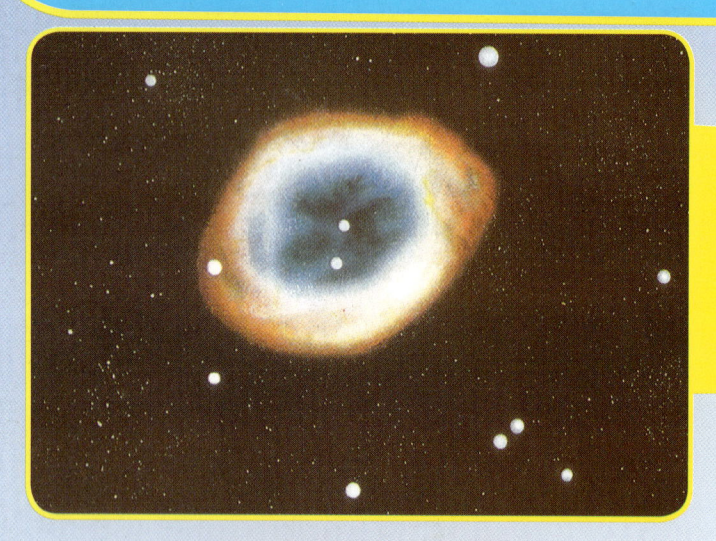

The Ring Nebula in Lyra, the most famous of the planetary nebulas. It is fairly easy to see with a telescope.

Stars with a mass similar to the Sun end their lives as white dwarfs after losing their wrapping. The density of a white dwarf is very high and it starts to cool very slowly, becoming darker and darker.

The Helix Nebula is a spectacular example of a planetary nebula. An old star has released a reddish hydrogen gas bubble 1, which can be seen in the form of a ring, with spiral branches. The nebula appears to be empty inside 2 because only the edges of the gas bubble can be seen. The hot, dense nucleus of the star is exposed by the expulsion of the gas bubble and appears as a blue star 3 in the geometric centre of the nebula.

Supernovas, the great fireworks

Not all stars end their lives as quietly as the white dwarfs. Massive stars, with much more matter than the Sun, continue a more complex evolution and finish their existence in a far more spectacular way. The nucleus of these stars is so compressed and hot that more nuclear reactions can occur. When such a star has used up all of its hydrogen, the nucleus becomes compressed and heats up until the carbon reacts bringing about heavier elements. When the carbon has run out, a similar process begins. These different phases happen quickly, because the new nuclear reactions produce less energy each time. Toward the end, the star begins to acquire a structure of layers, with the nucleus being made up of iron.

When it is no longer possible to obtain more energy from the iron, the star's centre collapses in on itself and the whole star explodes in one great, un-imaginable bang. This explosion can produce a glow of more than one hundred million Suns. We call such an explosion a *supernova*. Most of the star's matter disperses into space. The explosion produces a rapidly expanding nebula. The Crab nebula in the constellation Taurus is the remains of a supernova that Chinese astronomers saw in 1054.

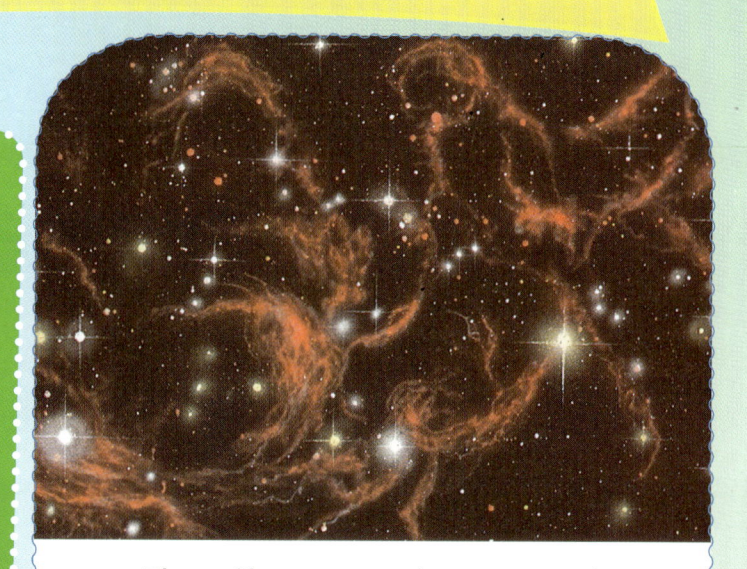

These filaments are the remains of a supernova explosion that happened more than 10,000 years ago in the constellation Vela, in the southern hemisphere.

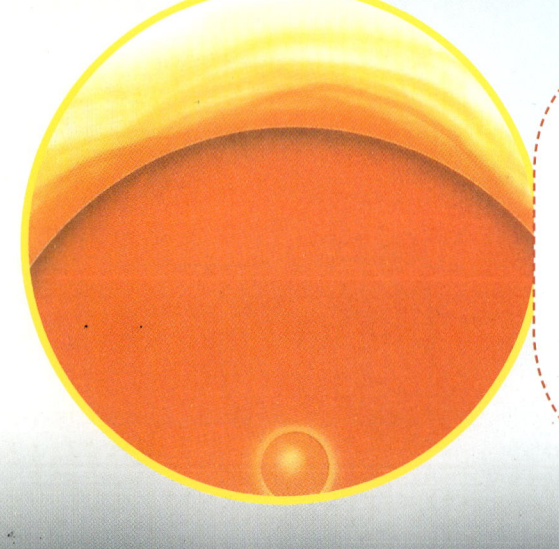

A star just before it explodes as a supernova. It is formed of successive layers of lighter elements: iron in the centre, then silicon, magnesium, sulphur, oxygen, neon, carbon, helium, and finally, a hydrogen wrapping. Nuclear reactions that take place between each pair of layers transform one element into another.

The Crab nebula in the constellation Taurus. It is the remains of supernova explosion observed in 1054 by Chinese astronomers. A large star exploded 1, hurling part of its matter into space. The nebula's filaments 2 are expanding at a great speed through the interstellar medium. Recently in 1987, a relatively close supernova, in the Great Magellanic Cloud, was studied for the first time.

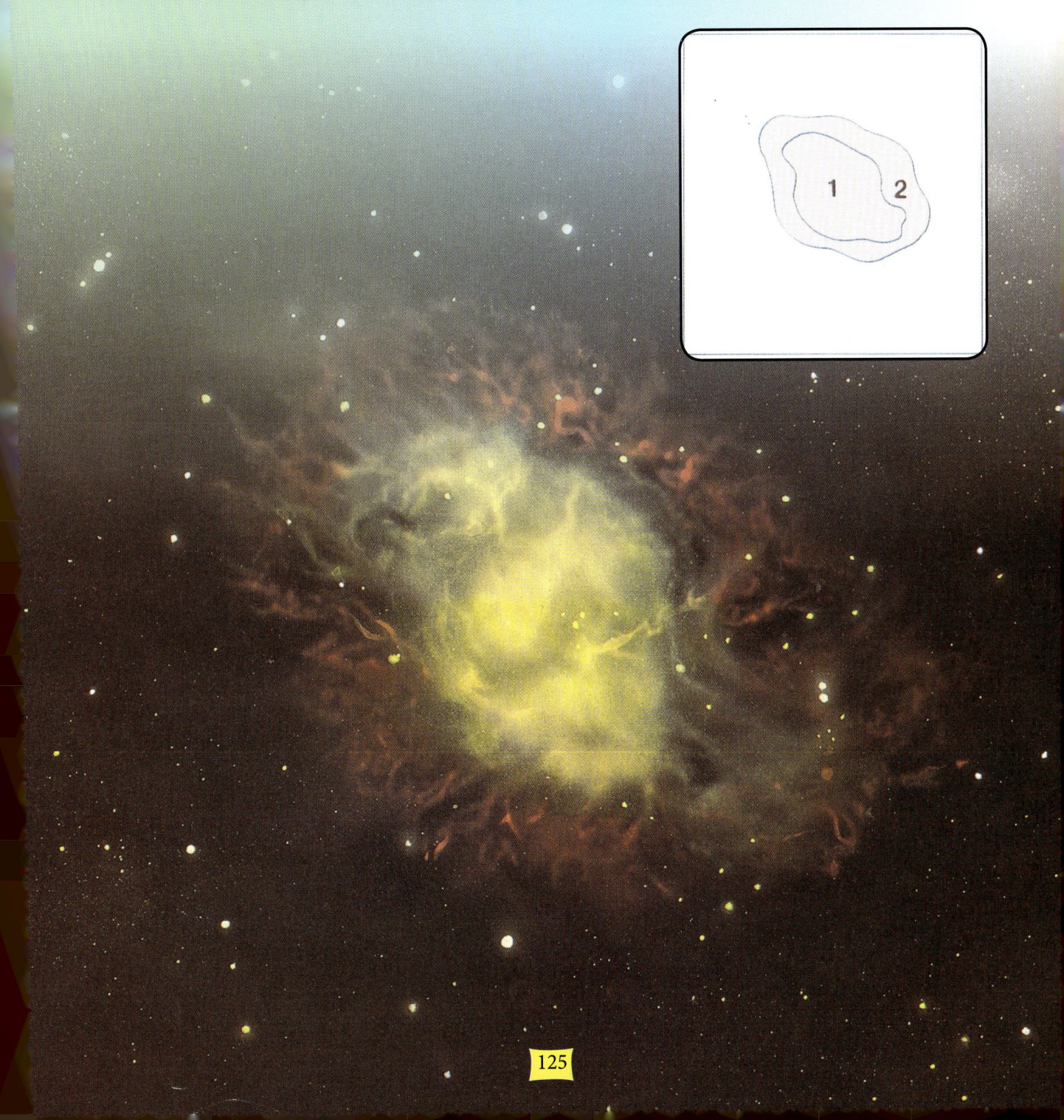

DO BLACK HOLES EXIST?

What happens when a star's nucleus contains an enormous quantity of matter? The neutron star's interior cannot support its own weight so it begins to compress into itself and collapses even further. But, unlike the other processes in a star's evolution, in this case a surprising thing happens. The star is condemned to totally collapse under its own weight. Its diameter begins to reduce at the same time that its density increases. There is nothing known in nature that is capable of opposing such an intense gravitational force. How does this process end? Surprisingly, it can be said that it never ends. When the force of gravity is very intense, the effects predicted by the theory of relativity become important, particularly the shrinking of time. We see that the process continuously becomes slower, in such a way that we can never see it end. There are other curious effects that have to do with this theory. At a certain point, gravity is so intense that even light cannot escape from the star in contraction. This is a **black hole**.

Although black holes have never been observed, it is believed that they exist. If in the case of a binary star system, where two stars are close together, one of the objects is a black hole and the other is a giant, a part of the giant's matter will be trapped by the black hole. The matter will begin falling toward the black hole and will heat up considerably and emit X rays.

If an unwary astronaut approached a black hole, the astronaut would become terribly stretched out. The black hole would pull the feet with much more force than the head.

A white dwarf star is about as big as the Earth. A neutron star has a diameter of only about 6 miles (10 kilometres), while a black hole is even more compressed.

It is suspected that there is a black hole in Cygnus X-1 1. Cygnus X-1 is a binary star system in which one of the stars is blue 2 and its companion, probably a black hole, is a very dense object containing a great mass. The blue star's matter is wrenched by this dense object and forms a disc around it 3. This matter heats up to a very high temperature while falling into the dense object, and emits radiation in the form of X rays 4.

The origin of the elements

There are about a hundred chemical elements in nature, which can be found in an isolated form or as part of the atmosphere, sea, or in the Earth's crust. Nitrogen can be found in the atmosphere, oxygen in seawater, silicon in rocks, and carbon in living beings.

All existing chemical elements, except hydrogen and helium, originated from inside stars. All the new elements were launched into space through the explosion of supernovas. Interstellar matter is enriched by these new chemicals. After a certain period of time, new stars are formed from interstellar material that has already been enriched by elements more complex than helium. Such matter eventually becomes part of the planets that are formed by a star. The origin of all Earth's atoms that are not hydrogen or helium is the stars, even the atoms of living beings, including ourselves. The matter that forms our bodies originated from the centre of a star.

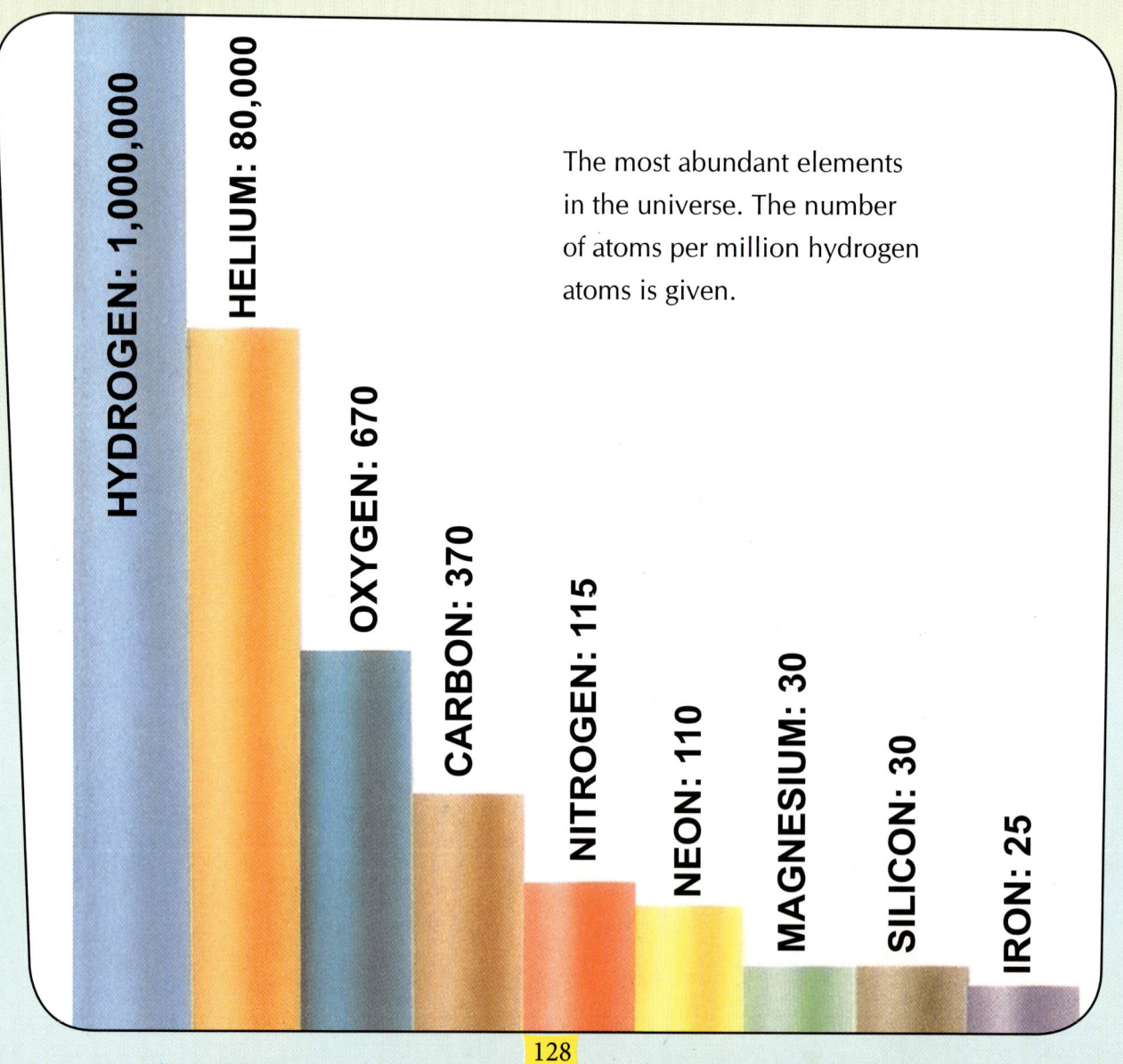

The most abundant elements in the universe. The number of atoms per million hydrogen atoms is given.

- HYDROGEN: 1,000,000
- HELIUM: 80,000
- OXYGEN: 670
- CARBON: 370
- NITROGEN: 115
- NEON: 110
- MAGNESIUM: 30
- SILICON: 30
- IRON: 25

The hydrogen atoms are formed by a proton and an electron. The atoms of helium have a nucleus containing two protons and two neutrons surrounded by two electrons. Carbon has six protons and six neutrons in its nucleus.

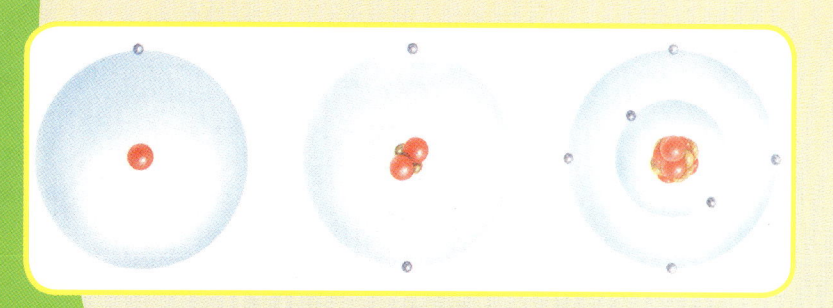

There are about a hundred different chemical elements of Earth. The atoms of the various elements are distinguished by the number of protons in the nucleus, which coincides with the number of electrons in the atom's shell. All elements, except hydrogen and helium, originated from the centre of a dense star. When the star explodes as a supernova, as you can see in this illustration, these elements are sent off into space. After sometime, they become new stars and planets that are formed from this interstellar material.

ACTIVITY. HOW MANY STARS ARE THERE?

To look at the night sky, we have to choose a place far from the city or town lights, and wait for a clear night, without clouds or fog. Once our eyes become adapted to the dark, we can observe this great spectacle. Although it is no surprise, it is always breathtaking. There are so many stars, it seems as if they could fall on our heads at any moment. If the question has any meaning, how many stars are there? A better way to put the question might be: How many stars can we see with our eyes? All the stars we can see belong to our galaxy, the Milky Way galaxy, which contains about 100 billion stars. But even with the biggest telescopes we can see only a small number of them, those that are closest to the Sun. By looking with the naked eye, we can see only the brightest stars, up to the sixth magnitude. In all, that would make a few thousand, about 6,000 if conditions are really excellent.

Counting stars with the naked eye seems to be an impossible job. But it can be done in a simpler way that is a lot of fun. Cut a hole with a diameter of about 5 inches (12 cm) in a piece of cardboard. Tie a string to the cardboard and make a knot about 12 inches (30 cm) from the card. If you hold the card so that the string is straight and perpendicular to your face, with the knot near your eye, you will see about 1% of the celestial sphere through the hole. Point the hole toward the sky and count the stars you see through it. Do the same in a total of ten different directions. Add up the number of stars you have counted in each direction and multiply the sum by ten. The answer will be the number of visible stars in the whole sky.

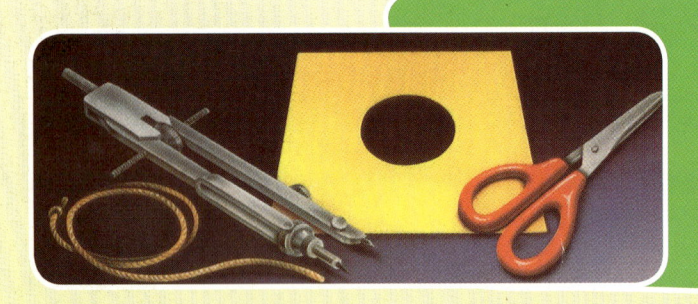

In order to do this activity you will need a piece of cardboard, a compass, a pair of scissors, and a piece of string. Use the compass to draw a circle with a diameter of about 5 inches (12 cm) on the cardboard. Then use the scissors to cut it out.

You have to look at the sky through the hole in the cardboard in ten different directions. Count the number of stars you see through the hole and multiply your answer by 10.

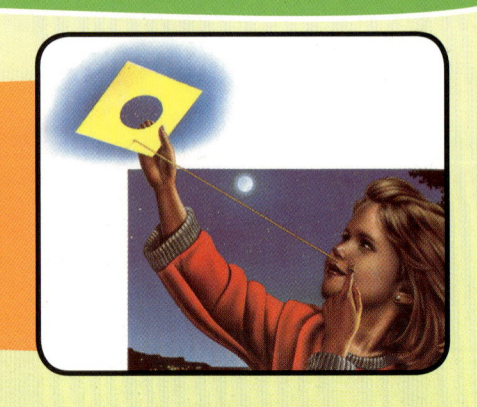

130

GALAXIES

Now that you know about the stars, it will interest you to learn about the galaxies. The stars we see at night sky belong to a huge spiral-shaped collection of stars called the Galaxy. Interesting isn't it? Take a look and seek out your queries as this chapter holds all the answers in the most enticing way.

The Night Sky

Tonight, before you go to bed, have a look at the night sky. You will see that the stars cover it more or less like a blanket. No one part of the sky seems to contain more stars than any other. But if you had a telescope or a pair of binoculars you would be able to look at the sky in detail. You would discover that the stars often appear in groups called **star clusters**. Large groups are known as **globular clusters** and consist of up to a million stars packed extremely close together in the shape of a ball. The stars that form globular clusters are old and reddish.

The Milky Way

On a dark night when the sky is clear, a faint white band can be seen stretching across the sky from horizon to horizon. This is the Milky Way. The famous astronomer, Galileo, was the first person to look closely at the Milky Way through a telescope. He noticed that its hazy brightness comes from a great accumulation of faint stars that are not visible to the naked eye.

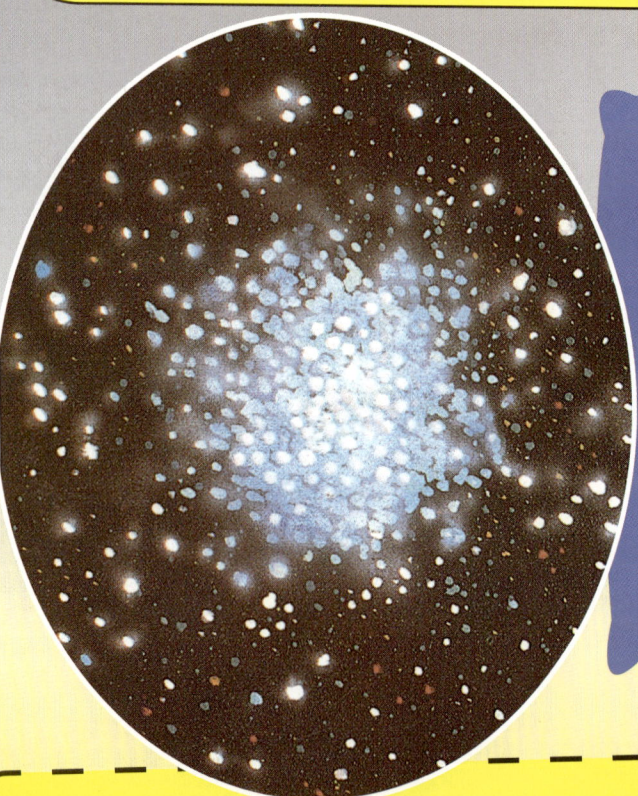

A Disc-Shaped System

So we know that the stars are not distributed evenly across the sky. Instead, they cluster together to form a disc-shaped system, which includes our Sun and Solar System. When we look up at the night sky in a direction at right angles to this disc, we can only see a few stars. But if we look along the flat surface of the disc, we can see a great accumulation of stars. This is the luminous band called the Milky Way.

Globular clusters are made up of old red stars closely packed together. If we use a small telescope, we can see the brightest globular clusters, many of which are found in the direction of the constellation Sagittarius in the southern hemisphere.

This image shows how globular clusters are distributed in a halo around the centre of our Galaxy.

The Milky Way [1] is a faint whitish band made up of the accumulated light of a large number of distant stars which cannot be seen by the naked eye. This band stretches across the sky and passes through the constellations of Cassiopeia and Cygnus when seen from the northern hemisphere, and Sagittarius and the Southern Cross in the southern sky. The coming together of stars in this band shows that the stars form a disc-shaped system which includes our Sun and Solar system.

The Milky Way

Our Galaxy: The Milky Way

By looking at the white band of the Milky Way, astronomers, have worked out that the Sun and its planetary system belong to a **planar** system made up of a large number of stars. This system is called a Galaxy. Our Galaxy is called the Milky Way, the same name that is given to the white band that we can see in the sky. Our Sun belongs to the Milky Way galaxy. It is one of the 1,00,000 million stars which make up our Galaxy.

The Galactic Disc

Our Galaxy is very flat. Most of the stars are concentrated in a plane called the galactic disc. The Sun is one of the stars in this disc and is situated far away from the centre, about 30,000 **light-years** away. It is closer to the edge of the disc than the centre. From our Solar System, we can only see the stars closest to us because of **matter** between the stars which absorbs light and prevents us from seeing the bright centre of the Galaxy.

A Spiral-Shaped Galaxy

The stars in the galactic disc revolve around the centre of the Galaxy following more or less circular orbits. Our Sun, for example, takes 220 million years to complete one orbit around the Galaxy. Since it was formed, the Sun has made more than 20 journeys around the Galaxy. The galactic disc has a spiral-shaped structure. Stars are being formed at this very moment in its spiral arms.

A large group of nebulous stars made of gas and dust is concentrated in the disc of the Milky Way.

The Milky Way, as well as giving visible light, also gives out radio waves which are particularly strong along the galactic disc.

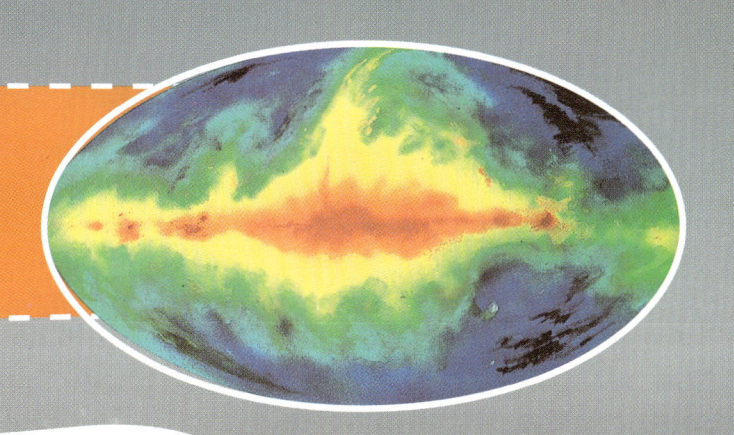

The disc of the Milky Way is over 1,00,000 light years in diameter. In the middle of the disc is a central bulge [1] or galactic nucleus which is the centre of the Galaxy. The galactic disc is spiral-shaped [2], but this is very difficult to see from inside the Milky Way. The spiral probably has four arms emerging from the nucleus. These arms hold a large group of newly-formed stars. The Sun is close to one of these spiral arms.

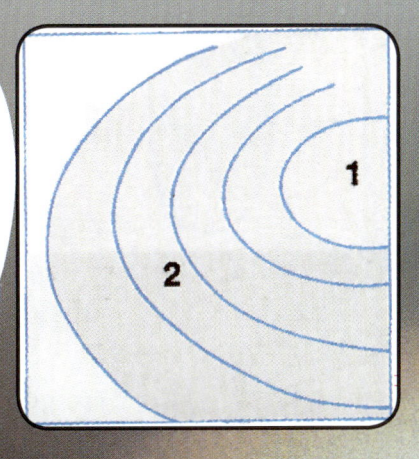

Dust and gas nebulae

The stars of the galactic disc are quite young because in this part of the Galaxy, in the spiral arms, new stars are being formed all the time. The stars are formed from the interstellar material that exists in space. This material is made up of mainly hydrogen and small dust particles. About 10% of the material in the Galaxy has not formed into stars, but exists instead as interstellar material.

Interstellar Dust

On Earth, we can only see stars up to a few thousand light years away from our Solar System. This is because interstellar dust and gas absorbs most of the visible light, making it impossible to see the centre of the Galaxy.

Interstellar Gas

The interstellar gas is not visible under normal conditions. But when it is heated by the light of a bright star, the gas gives off a pink light, characteristic of hydrogen. This brilliant gas forms nebulae that contain young bright stars. It is these stars that make the gas give out light.

The Trifid nebula in the Sagittarius constellation is divided up by three dark bands of dust. The gas appears to shine when it is heated by recently formed stars.

The bright nebula in the constellation of Orion can be seen with a pair of binoculars or a small telescope. New stars are formed in the thickest parts of the nebula.

The region around the star Rho Ophiuci [1] displays a rich mixture of all types of nebula. We can see a dark nebula made of dust which blocks out the light of the stars behind it [2]; various blue nebulae that reflect the light of the stars [3]; and hot gas nebulae that have a characteristic pink colour [4]. There is also a globular star cluster, tightly packed together [5].

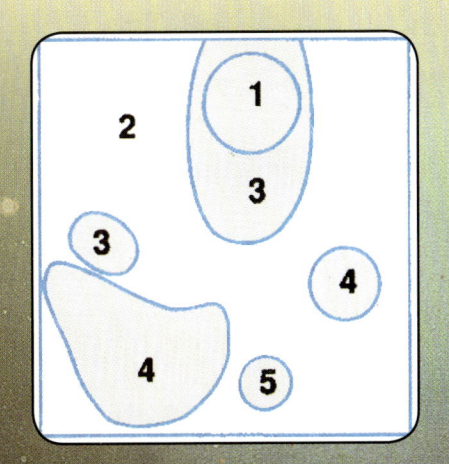

OUR NEIGHBOURING GALAXIES

What is beyond the Milky Way? For many years scientists thought that there was nothing beyond our Galaxy. They thought that our Galaxy, the Milky Way, was the entire Universe.

Nebulous Objects

Scientists had noticed, however, that there were various nebulous objects in the sky which had a curious spiral structure. The Andromeda constellation was one of these nebulous objects. Some astronomers began to think that Andromeda could be a galaxy similar to the Milky Way but situated a great distance away.

Two Million Light years

When the large Mount Palomar telescope was built, scientists saw that Andromeda is made up of stars and is, in fact, a galaxy, which lies two million light-years away. We now know there are over 1000 million galaxies in the Universe, each one similar to our Milky Way and made up of thousands of millions of stars.

The Magellanic Clouds are two small galaxies which are satellites of the Milky Way. The group of galaxies near the Milky Way is called the Local Group.

The Andromeda galaxy [1] is a large spiral galaxy similar to our Milky Way and, in space terms, quite close to us. There are other galaxies, besides Andromeda, which are our neighbours. This group of galaxies is called the Local Group. The most important members of the Local Group are the Milky Way and Andromeda which are both large spiral galaxies. The others are much smaller galaxies, which we can only see because they are so close.

The Shapes of Galaxies

We cannot see our own Galaxy from the outside, so it is very difficult to know exactly what shape it is. We do know that the Milky Way is very similar to the Andromeda galaxy, which is also a spiral galaxy. Not all the galaxies are like Andromeda. The Magellanic Clouds, for example, are small, irregular galaxies which have no particular shape.

Elliptical Galaxies

Many other galaxies are spherical or oval-shaped, like a rugby ball. These are called elliptical galaxies. The stars that form the elliptical galaxies are not grouped in the form of a disc. They also tend to be red and old. Elliptical galaxies do not spin as a whole, although the stars in them follow long stretched-looking orbits around the centre of the galaxy. They seem to be very old, but it is not known exactly how they began.

Spiral Galaxies

The spiral galaxies are very different from the elliptical galaxies. Most of the stars in a spiral galaxy are brighter and are arranged in flat disc that has lots of shining arms. The spiral arms may come directly from the centre of the galaxy or from a short bar in the central part of the galaxy. In this case, the galaxies are called barred spirals.

Despite their differences, galaxies can be classified into broad groups according to their shape. Scientific classification splits them into five groups: elliptical galaxies [1], normal closed spirals [2], normal open spirals [3], and barred spirals, closed [4] and open [5].

Elliptical galaxies [1] can be round or oval-shaped like a lentil or a rugby ball. The stars in spiral galaxies [2] are grouped in a flat disc that has several spiral arms [3]. It is in these spiral arms that new stars are constantly formed out of interstellar material, which is made up of mostly gas and dust. Spiral galaxies spin around their centre, although not all of them move in the same way: the stars closest to the middle move faster than the ones further away.

Galaxies in Contact

In space terms, the galaxies are all quite close together. For example, the Milky Way has a diameter of around 1,00,000 light years, while the Andromeda galaxy, which is close to the Milky Way, is at a distance of only about 20 times this diameter. The Magellanic Clouds are even closer. So astronomers can say that the nearby galaxies are almost touching. By comparison, the stars that make up these galaxies are huge distances apart in relation to their own size.

Clusters of Galaxies

Galaxies tend to gather into a group. This is called a **cluster of galaxies.** The Local Group, for example, is the galaxy cluster that contains the Milky Way. Sometimes clusters of galaxies are, in turn, pulled together by gravity to form **superclusters,** which are the largest known structures in the Universe.

Collisions in Space

So it is not too surprising that collisions between galaxies are quite frequent. Two galaxies do not need to actually collide in order to affect one another. The **gravitational pull** of a galaxy may influence all the galaxies that are close to it. The spiral arms that some galaxies have could be a result of the gravitational disturbances caused by other galaxies.

A collision between two galaxies begins when they come so close to one another that their gravitational pull draws them into each other.

The stars that are torn from each galaxy form long, flowing strips that stretch over a great distance.

When the collision begins, the stars on the outside are ripped away from the main body of each galaxy.

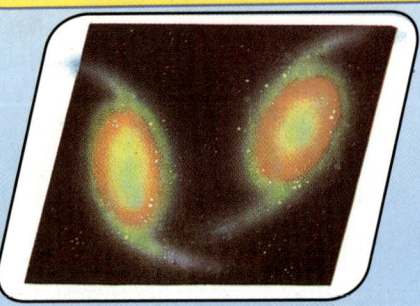

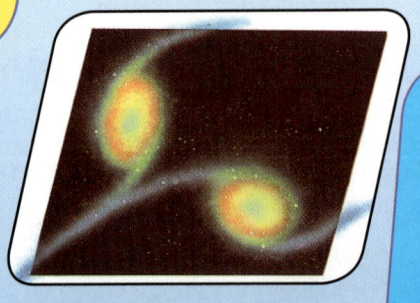

Finally, the material torn from the two galaxies takes the shape of long arms sticking out from the main body of the galaxies.

When two galaxies [1] come close to each other, the shape of both may change because the force of gravitational attraction pulls them closer together. Many galaxies have strange outlines that look like rings or long arms [2]. These are the result of a collision between two galaxies. But the stars are so far apart that two galaxies may pass through each other without any of the stars in the galaxies actually crashing into each other.

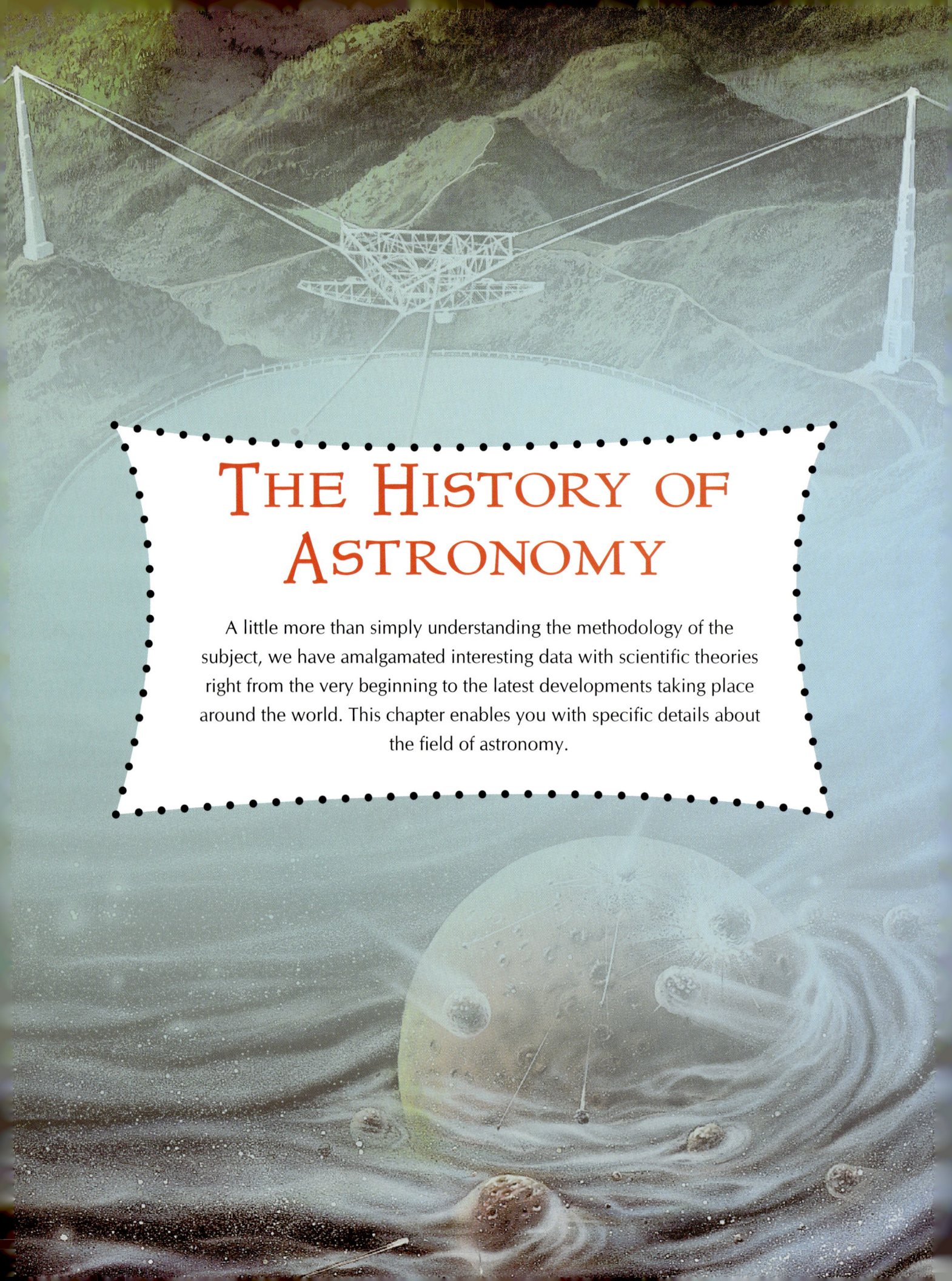

The History of Astronomy

A little more than simply understanding the methodology of the subject, we have amalgamated interesting data with scientific theories right from the very beginning to the latest developments taking place around the world. This chapter enables you with specific details about the field of astronomy.

The History of Astronomy

Astronomy was long connected to astrology which is devoted to interpreting human destiny by the stars. The first astronomers were priests who worked in the temples and devised predictions about the future, and also created the bases of this science. The Greeks were the first ones who entirely separated astronomy and religion. That is when the history of astronomical science began.

Babylonia

As early as 5,000 years ago the inhabitants of Babylon (modern-day Iraq), recorded on their tables the regularity of certain celestial phenomena, such as the changes in the phases of the Moon and the movement of the Sun to different heights at different times of the years. In efforts to predict the future in such practical matters as the flooding of rivers, they would consult the stars, and in order to locate them they devised the first precise measurements of their passage through the heavens.

China

Three thousand years ago the Chinese constructed astronomical observatories that were very sophisticated for the time. They divided the year into four seasons that were marked off by the solstices (in summer and winter) and the equinoxes (in the spring and fall). They divided the heavens into twenty-eight areas that were related to the various positions of the Moon. As early as the middle of the eleventh century they observed a nova, the source of the Cancer nebula.

The Chaldeans invented the water clock to measure time in their observations.

India

Around the same time when the Chinese were building the first astronomical observatories, Indian scientists were studying mathematics, which they related to the stars. Astronomy grew out of the old religion of the country, but the necessity of knowing the position of the heavenly bodies soon linked it to mathematics.

The Indian astronomical observatory of Jantar Mantar in Jaipur, India.

143

Astronomers of Pre-Columbian America

The Mayas were great mathematicians who used their knowledge to create a complex and very precise calendar. It was very important in predicting the times of harvest and rains. In Mayan cities astronomical observatories were erected next to temples dedicated to the gods; the priests used the observatories to study the movement of the heavenly bodies and make their predictions of eclipses, the movement of the stars, and the length of the year. The Aztecs and the Incas also had very precise numerical systems, which constituted one of the bases of their social systems.

The Mayan pyramid El Adivino in Uxmal, Mexico.

The Greeks

The Greeks were excellent mathematicians who applied their knowledge to geometry and astronomy. Much of their knowledge is still used as the basis of science today. Thales of Miletus, Pythagoras, and Aristotle were among the thinkers who established that foundation. The Greek astrologers were able to calculate the radius of the Earth, which they already perceived as a sphere. They also calculated very precisely the periods of the planets and many stars.

Around 2,500 years ago the Greeks were the first to completely separate science from religion, thereby freeing up thought and making scientific advances possible.

Ptolemy believed that the Earth was the centre of the universe and that the Sun and the planets revolved around it.

Copernicus, Kepler, and Galileo

During the sixteenth century these three astronomers did basic work that completely transformed the concept of the universe; building on the knowledge of the Greeks, they provided the definitive impulse to astronomy as a science. After many calculations and observations, Copernicus declared that the Earth was not the centre of the universe, but rather that it and the rest of the planets move around the Sun. Kepler, with his laws of physics, demonstrated that Copernicus was right. Galileo likewise defended his ideas, which he also backed up with his observations; he conducted them with the help of the telescope that he invented.

Galileo Gallilei studying the skies.

The Hubble space telescope.

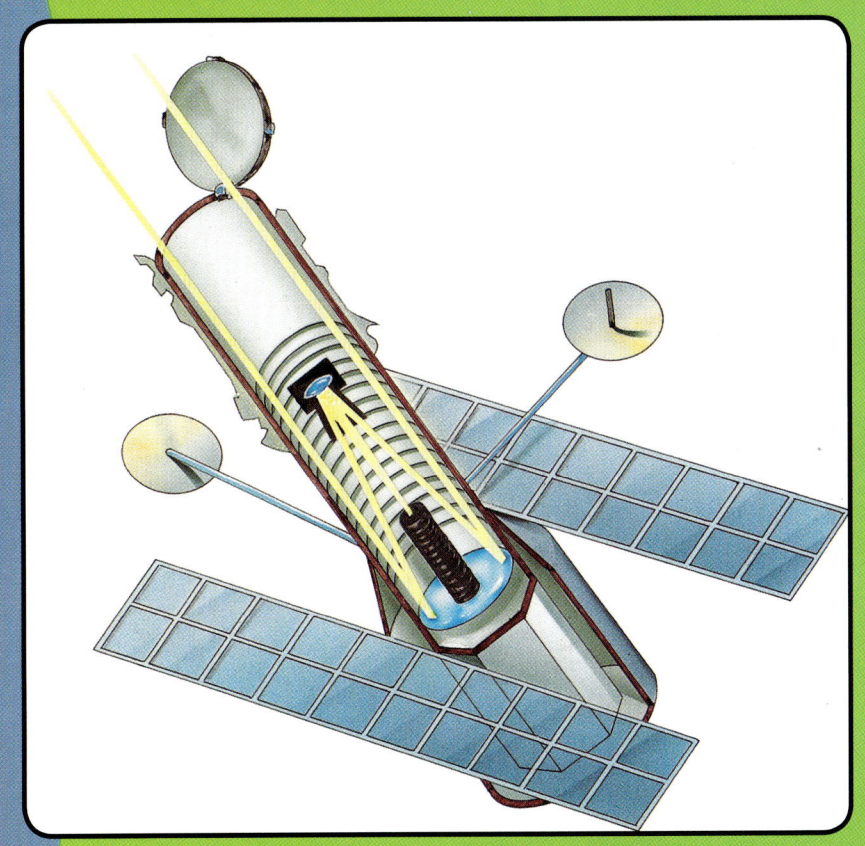

Modern Astronomy

Ever since the time of Copernicus, astronomy has been evolving rapidly. His discoveries tell us that we are merely one planet belonging to a small star located on the outer edge of one of the thousands of galaxies that make up the universe. Enormous optical telescopes have been constructed to prove that, and they make it possible to view stars located millions of light-years away from the Earth. Radio telescopes were invented to see farther, beyond the limits of optical instruments, and radio telescopes have been invented in order to observe the heavens clearly without interference from the Earth's atmosphere. In recent years artificial satellites have been launched, and space stations have been constructed and equipped with astronomical instruments. Spaceships now travel throughout the entire solar system, and they provide us with a unique view of the universe.

ASTRONOMY

Astronomy is what we call the science that is devoted to the study of heavenly bodies, plus all the general phenomena that takes place outside our planet. Now-a-days it is a science that makes use of complicated technology; it requires difficult mathematical calculations, and it involves travel in space, but its origins were very different.

The first astronomers lived about 5,000 years ago in Mesopotamia. They were priests who contemplated the sky and managed to predict eclipses. In addition, by determining the duration of the phases of the moon and the seasons—which had never before been measured, even though they were a permanent part of everyone's life—they improved the agricultural practices employed at that time. This seemingly small advance meant that the work in the fields could be linked to the cycle of the seasons and that it was possible to predict changes.

However, these astronomer-priests were entirely ignorant of the mechanisms that governed those celestial phenomena, and they interpreted them as interventions by the gods. In that way, astronomy was born in close association with religion and mythology.

The ancient Greeks, who created science as we recognize it today, also studied the sky and devised an explanation for the mysterious phenomenon of eclipses. In addition, with the aid of their calculations on heavenly bodies, they were able for the first time to determine the precise radius of the Earth. Other people in ancient times, notably the Indians and the Egyptians, also devoted themselves to this branch of knowledge, and for the same reasons. Ptolemy used his observations and measurements to establish an overall system in which the Earth was the absolute centre and all the planets and other heavenly bodies rotated around it. This idea remained in force as dogma through nearly 1,500 years.

In medieval Europe, astronomy stagnated with no new developments; but in America the Aztec astronomers carried out minute observations of the heavens that allowed them to establish very precise calendars and perform mathematical calculations relative to the heavenly bodies. Around the sixteenth century the situation began to change. Copernicus was the first one to take in the new ideas from scientific thought that were being generated, and after twenty-five years of observations, he arrived at the conclusion that it was the Sun, rather than the Earth, that was the centre of the universe. This was a completely revolutionary idea for the time, and it also marked the birth of modern astronomy.

It is estimated that some fifteen billion years have passed since the formation of the universe with a huge explosion known as the **Big Bang**.

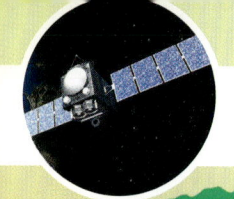

MODERN ASTRONOMY

At the time of Copernicus the heavens came under new scrutiny using scientific criteria and new instruments that were being invented. Telescopes finally made it possible to make scientific observations. Some great names from these times are Tycho Brahe, Kepler, Galileo, and Newton, who contributed enormously to the abandonment of the idea that the Earth was the centre of the universe, thereby confirming the ideas of Copernicus.

As improvements were made in the instruments used for observing the skies, new celestial bodies were discovered, including the satellites of various planets, and it became possible to calculate the orbit of comets. It finally became possible to confirm with certainty the orbit of the planets that make up the solar system, and to begin studying other systems. In that way, astronomy situated our planet in a universe that kept expanding as more distant worlds were explored. We will see what the overall solar system is like, and we will visit each of the nine known planets that make it up (including our own), as well as the Moon and the asteroid belt. Spaceships have reached some of these celestial bodies and have taken samples of their soil; as a result, ever since the middle of the twentieth century we have known data that a mere century ago seemed absolutely impossible to obtain.

A comet is a heavenly body that has a very distinct appearance and behaviour, and that travels through the solar system.

But our solar system is not the only one, and our star, the Sun, is just a medium-sized one located at the edge of our galaxy, which is one of many that make up the universe. Astronomy studies all these heavenly bodies and the phenomena that occur outside our small planet; these include comets, galaxies and nebulae, dwarf stars, supernovas, and the mysterious black holes.

The nine planets of the solar system, from left to right: Mercury, Venus, Earth, Mars, Jupiter, Saturn, Uranus, Neptune, and Pluto

Astronomical Instruments

Professional astronomers use powerful computers to do their calculations, and complicated mathematical formulas to establish their theories; they also use enormous telescopes to observe outer space. But amateur astronomers can study the skies without such advanced methods, using anything from strong binoculars, which allow viewing the surface of the Moon in greater detail, to small telescopes that make it possible to view some distant galaxies. These instruments are all you need to enjoy this hobby. In addition to the telescopes that are used for observing the light emitted by heavenly bodies and stars—in other words, optical instruments—the discovery of radio and other types of waves has opened up new fields of astronomy. Thus, many of the telescopes currently used in observatories use radio waves that are emitted from the farthest areas of the universe, and that take millions of years to reach us here on Earth. This branch of astronomy goes by the name of radio astronomy; it allows astronomers and scientists to reach more distant areas than those that are accessible using traditional optical telescopes.

In the section devoted to instruments used for observation we will also dedicate some space to the great astronomers who have made observations throughout the centuries and established theories that make it possible for us to have a more complete idea of what the universe is today.

Astronautics

Astronautics is a set of very diverse disciplines that are focused primarily on space travel beyond our planet. Even though this pursuit has a history, it's been around for scarcely half a century; nevertheless, it has added tremendously to our knowledge of astronomy and has contributed significantly to progress in many daily activities. Some aspects of astronautics are as spectacular as putting a man on the Moon, or obtaining images of the surface of the planet Mars, but there are others as well that we scarcely realize, and that make our lives easier. These primarily involve communications. Nowadays, television reaches all parts of the globe thanks to the man-made satellites that rotate around the Earth. Weather forecasting is more accurate, and shows real maps with the location of weather fronts and their movement, thanks to the photos sent back by meteorological satellites. Cellular phones, which are so common today, allow us to speak with any point on the planet, thanks once again to these communications satellites. We will see what the first attempts to launch objects into space were like, with the successes and failures. But all of these attempts produced results that allowed another step forward.

Just a little more than twenty years passed from the time of the first man-made satellite to the arrival of the first man to step onto the surface of the Moon; this is a very short period of time when we compare it to the centuries it took to gather the knowledge that made that voyage possible.

Astronautics offers a fascinating world of spaceships that are ever larger and more powerful, the shuttles that transport astronauts from a base on Earth to the space stations in orbit around the planet, and the space stations themselves, where the astronauts remain for months carrying out observations and experiments to make even longer journeys possible.

The Future of Astronomy and Astronautics

The speed at which advances in astronomy and astronautics take place makes it difficult to predict the future, but we will take a look at some outlines of the projects that are being prepared for the coming years. Bases on the Moon are already a possibility, and permanent space stations are a reality that we can read about in newspapers on a daily basis. Travel to nearby planets is one of the projects underway, but exploration of the most distant ones and those beyond our solar system will be reserved for unmanned spaceships. But scientific advances also produce a broad diversity of applications, so there are already some travel agencies that are beginning to organize trips to the Moon and stays on our satellite, where they are planning hotels and small cities. Although until a few years ago the majority of these plans were just science fiction, today they are starting to turn into reality (since the first space tourist took a flight in 2001); they will have repercussions in daily life for all of us because of the new uses that will be made of the technical resources needed to make them happen.

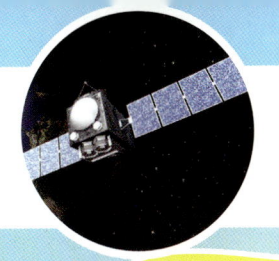

Great astronomers of ancient times

Astronomy did not exist as such in ancient times. The priests were the ones whose duty it was to observe the sky; they searched in the stars for answers to their daily questions. Still, the great Greek thinkers, the founders of science, were the first ones to study the sky and establish the bases of astronomy.

Aristotle

This Greek philosopher was born in Stagira in 384 B.C. and died in Calcedonia in 322 B.C. He was one of the main thinkers of ancient times and was dedicated to botany, zoology, psychology, medicine, physics, and astronomy, as well as philosophy. Even though the sciences were just one area to which he didn't devote many of his works, his authority as a thinker was so great that for centuries his conclusions in these fields were considered irrefutable. Aristotle maintained that the Earth was a sphere that remained in a fixed position in space and was the centre of the universe. The other planets, the stars, the Moon, and the Sun revolved around it. He proved that through philosophical reasoning, and since no one had access to modern mathematical knowledge or instruments of observation, it was impossible to contradict him. The things that Aristotle said, in other fields as well as astronomy, were considered absolute truth for almost a thousand years.

Aristotle wrote About the Sky, where he addressed topics in astronomy.

In 335 B.C. Aristotle founded the Lyceum in the city of Athens.

Hipparchus of Nicae

This Greek scientist lived during the second century B.C.; we don't know many details about his life, but he is considered the founder of scientific astronomy. He did some important calculations on the movement of the Sun and the Moon, and described the Moon's orbit with some precision. One of his main works was the first catalogue of stars. He succeeded in identifying a little more than a thousand stars; he classified them into six categories according to their brightness, and he invented the method that is still in use today.

Eratosthenes

The Greek geographer, philosopher, and astronomer Eratosthenes was born in Cyrene in 284 B.C. and died in Alexandria in 192 B.C. He was a clever mathematician who performed many very precise calculations to determine geographic distances. Among other things, he invented a type of grid with perpendicular axes that could be used to locate towns and cities when their distances were known. He was director of the library of Alexandria. One of his most important accomplishments was calculating the circumference of the Earth. He observed that on the spring equinox (March 21) the Sun was reflected on the bottom of the wells in the city of Aswan, but in Alexandria (which was located on the same meridian but a little farther south) there was a little shadow. He deduced that was due to the curvature of the Earth. Then he measured the distance between the two cities and determined the radius of the Earth very accurately.

Claudius Ptolemaeus (Ptolemy)

This Greek philosopher, mathematician, and astronomer was born and lived in Alexandria in the second century B.C. He wrote a monumental work in thirteen volumes entitled Sintaxis Matematica, in which he assembled all the knowledge about astronomy that existed at that time. In addition, he created astronomical tables and an important work of cartography that was used to make the most accurate maps of his time. He also made a catalogue that includes 1,200 stars. His main contribution to this science is the planetary model he created and described in five books. His concept of the universe was adopted by astronomers and lasted for more than thirteen centuries.

Ptolemy's Model of the Universe

The system proposed by Ptolemy considered that the Earth was the centre of the universe. He maintained that the Earth was a sphere and that the Moon, the planets, the Sun, and the stars were arranged around it, revolving in precise orbits. In order to explain observed irregularities, Ptolemy invented a complicated set of corrective calculations.

Modern Astronomers

The ideas about the universe that had been conceived by the classical Greek astronomers were considered irrefutable truths for several centuries. The fifteenth century produced the first great revolution when Copernicus stated that the Earth was not the centre of the universe. From that time onwards astronomy began its transformation into the science that we know today.

Nicholas Copernicus

A Polish astronomer, Copernicus devised some very useful inventions. He was a careful analyst of all the theories known at that time, and he compared them with the most recent available information, and with his own observations. All this led him to conclude that the Earth was not the centre of the universe.

Copernicus assembled his theory in a work that was opposed by the Church, but he saw it published during his lifetime.

Copernicus maintained that the Earth and the other planets revolved around the Sun

Johannes Kepler

This German astronomer was born in Weil der Stadt on December 27, 1571, and died in Ratisbona on November 15, 1630. He worked as the imperial mathematician, but he always had great financial difficulties. He invented a telescope in order to carry out his observations more effectively, but he concentrated his work on mathematical calculations for the trajectories of the planets; this allowed him to devise his laws concerning their movement. Kepler's laws confirm that the planets move in elliptical orbits around the Sun, and the closer they are to it, the faster they move.

To come up with his laws, Kepler spent ten years studying the orbit of Mars.

Galileo Galilei

This Italian mathematician, astronomer, and physicist was born in Pisa on February 15, 1564, and died near Florence on January 8, 1642. He discovered the laws of the pendulum, constructed a hydrostatic balance, and invented a gas thermometer. In 1609 he constructed an improved telescope that magnified thirty times and that he used to study the stars. He made some very important contributions to astronomy, such as the discovery of sunspots, calculating the rotational period of the Sun, and determining that the stars are very far from our planet, and that the universe may be infinite. He was a great defender of the theory of Copernicus, and that led to a confrontation with the Church, which had declared that the Copernican ideas were heresy for denying that the Earth was the centre of the universe. The Inquisition denounced him and put him on trial, and in response to a threat of being sent to prison, in 1632 he was forced to renounce those theories; he was confined to house arrest, where he continued working with his disciples despite being half blind.

Galileo demonstrated that the Milky Way is not a cloud but a large number of stars.

Other discoveries of Galileo include the mountains on the Moon and four of Jupiter's satellites.

According to legend, after renouncing the Copernican theory in front of the judges of the Inquisition, Galileo asserted that "in spite of that (the Earth) does move."

Analyzing A Star

In 1814, the German physicist Joseph Fraunhofer observed that as the light from the Sun (or any other star) passed through a prism, black lines were produced (the spectrum of absorption), and that makes it possible to analyze the composition of any star.

In 1927, Georges Lemaître proposed a theory on the origin of the universe that later became known as the **Big Bang**.

Today's astronomers are able to study hundreds of millions of stellar systems located outside our galaxy.

Telescopes and other Instruments

Advances in astronomy are closely linked to the development of scientific instruments that make it possible to study the skies. Still, amateurs can carry out observations using very simple instruments. The instruments available for studying stars run the gamut from binoculars up to the large telescopes used in astronomical observatories.

A Simple Way to Count Stars

All the stars that we can see with the naked eye belong to our galaxy, the Milky Way. There is a very simple way to calculate about how many we can see on any night. Cut out a 4 3/4-inch (12 cm) circle on a piece of cardboard and hold it 12 inches (30 cm) in front of your eyes; for that purpose you can tie on a 12-inch (30 cm) string and keep it stretched tight between your face and the cardboard. The hole in the cardboard makes it possible to study 1 percent of the sky. You can count the stars you see through the hole and repeat the count ten times in different directions. By adding together the numbers thus obtained, you will have the number of stars in 10 percent of the celestial sphere. By multiplying by ten you will have calculated the number of stars.

To observe the sky effectively, you have to look for a place far from town to avoid reflections from the lights.

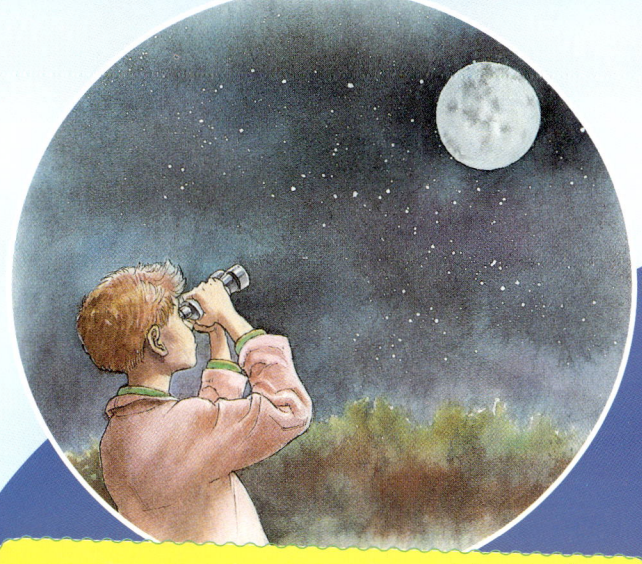

Binoculars

This optical instrument used for observing wild animals and looking at distant people and places can also be used for studying a fairly large number of stars and the surface of the Moon. With strong binoculars you can see a large number of craters, mountains, and "seas" on our satellite. The best type for astronomical observations is a 7 ¥ 50 (seven power with an objective lens of 50 mm diameter).

When you look at stars through binoculars, it is a good idea to rest your elbows on a firm support to reduce vibrations.

The Astronomical Telescope

This simple instrument, as it was used in ancient times, consists of a tube fitted with a magnifying lens in one end. Later it was discovered that the power could be increased by adding a second lens. Galileo perfected this arrangement and constructed a thirty-power telescope. The first lens provides a small image of the object under observation—the Moon, for example. The second lens, which is located in the eyepiece (through which the observer peers) magnifies that first image.

The Telescope

This instrument is an improvement on the earlier astronomical telescope; it contains more lenses that correct the defects produced in the image and increase the instrument's capacity. The two most important characteristics of telescope are their power and their luminosity. The former is a function of the relationship between the focal distance between the objective and ocular lenses. Luminosity depends on the diameter of the objective lens; the larger it is, the better the luminosity of the instrument.

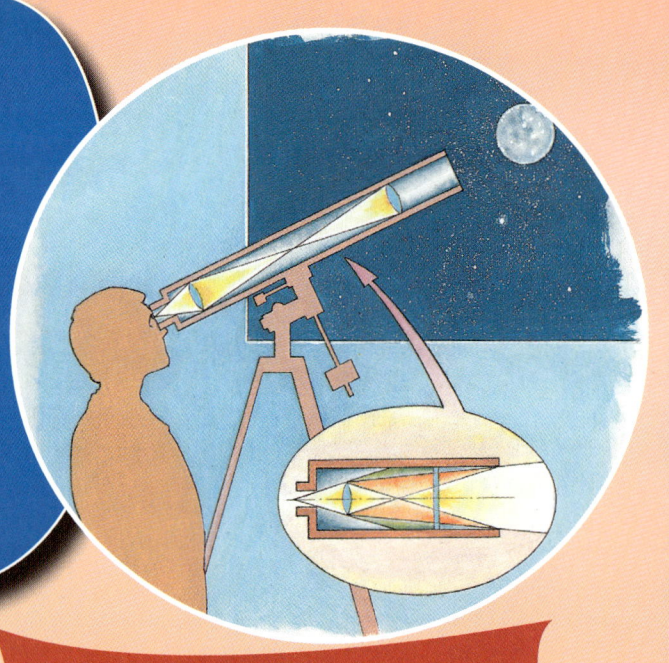

Resolution is the instrument's capacity to differentiate between two objects placed very close together. The human eye's power of resolution is referred to as visual acuity.

The image that is observed in the ocular lens of the astronomical lens appears upside down.

A telescope with a 1,000 mm focal length objective and a 10 mm ocular focal length yields a magnification of 100 power.

Modern Telescopes

Modern telescopes are large in size, and consist of many auxiliary features that allow them to be moved with great precision. In addition, instead of observing the image directly, the image is produced by reflection in a mirror. The light that enters the telescope is reflected in a concave mirror located at the bottom. The reflected image falls onto a flat mirror, and that is what is observed with the aid of the ocular lens.

Radio telescopes and spectrometres

Visible light makes it possible to see a great number of heavenly bodies, but there are many more that emit no light; they seem to be covered by interstellar dust that absorbs light, or they are so far away that the power of an optical telescope is not sufficient to detect them. As a result, astronomers use other types of electromagnetic radiation similar to radio waves. In addition, spectrometres make it possible to study the composition of heavenly bodies.

Radio Telescopes

In 1931, an engineer who was trying to find a way to improve radio reception and avoid static accidentally discovered that some static comes from space. Astronomers began to use this new medium to explore the sky. The result has been the discovery of many stars and other features of the universe. Light is just one part of the radiation that celestial bodies give off. The wavelength varies along a broad spectrum. Radio telescopes detect all the wavelengths that are not part of visible light. These telescopes are very large and consist mainly of a reflector in the shape of a concave mirror to concentrate the radiation in a central point where it is registered—in other words, the antenna. From there the signal is sent to an amplifier that treats it in such a way that it can be studied.

Radio telescopes are similar to the parabolic antennas that we use to view television channels transmitted by satellite, but they are much larger.

In order to produce a resolution of 1¢ a parabolic reflector 2,277 feet (690 m) in diameter is needed. The Arecibo (Puerto Rico) radio telescope has a parabolic antenna 990 feet (300 m) in diameter.

Spectrometres

When white solar light is made to pass through a glass prism, the light comes out the other side split into various colours. What happens is that the prism divides the beam of white light into each of its components or colours. Each colour has a different wavelength and is reflected on the faces of the prism at different angles. All these colours together constitutes what is known as the spectrum of solar light. Physicists have discovered that when a chemical element becomes incandescent it gives off a characteristic spectrum—in other words, one that is made up of different proportions of colours. As a result, if we know the spectrum of each element we can determine whether or not the light that comes in from any given location contains that element. This is the principle of spectrometry. A spectrometer is an instrument that analyzes the light that comes in from space (for example, from a star) and makes it possible to know what chemical elements it contains.

The prism decomposes white light into its various constituent colours. The wavelengths of the colours of solar light vary between .40 thousandths of a mm for purple and .70 thousandths of a mm for red.

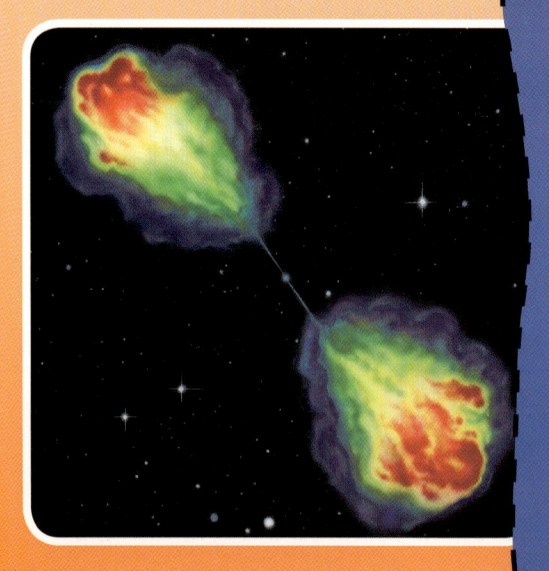

Interferometres and Radar

These two instruments are also used for studying the skies. Interferometres consist of two mirrors located at a certain distance from one another that reflect the image or the received radiation onto an optical telescope or a radio telescope to produce an interference image that improves its resolution capacity. Radar sends out a bundle of signals toward a celestial body (the Moon or a planet) and receives an echo that makes it possible to study the surface of that body and determine how far away it is. Many of these instruments are mounted on artificial satellites and spaceships, thereby increasing their efficiency by escaping the influence of the layers of air in the Earth's atmosphere.

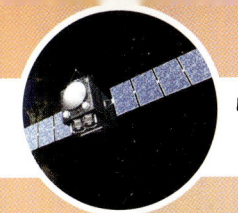

THE FIRST ATTEMPTS

In ancient times, humans were inseparably linked to the soil, but they still dreamed of flying. The sky was seen as a sphere that extended over the Earth and where the gods lived, but people still dreamed about going there. The dreams became a reality beginning in the nineteenth century. It became possible to fly, and in the middle of the twentieth century, people succeeded in launching objects outside the planet. Those were the first attempts to make that old dream come true.

Chinese

The Chinese invented gunpowder, and they quickly began to search for applications for this extraordinary product. The main uses to which they put it were military, since the possibility of destroying walls and launching projectiles, rudimentary though it was, is an important basis for any army. A hollow tube (such as a piece of bamboo) filled with powder and fitted with an opening in the rear, was propelled forward when the explosive was lit. By placing such a tube on end, it was possible to make it travel upward in a fairly straight line. That's how the first rocket came to be.

The fins of a rocket serve to stabilize it in flight by overcoming wobble and assuring a straight trajectory. Fireworks are an ancient application of gunpowder. They involve launching a small rocket into the air so that it explodes at a certain altitude and sends out coloured sparks in all directions.

Jules Verne

This French writer was born in 1828 and died in 1905. He was the author of many adventure books such as Around the World in Eighty Days, A Journey to the Centre of the Earth, and Twenty Thousand Leagues Under the Sea. In all his works he shows a great vision of the future accomplishments of science and technology. In one of these works he delves into space travel a full century before it became possible, performing many very precise calculations. That was in his book From the Earth to the Moon, in which a group of people are placed inside an enormous cannon ball and shot toward our satellite.

To leave the Earth

Among many other calculations, Verne determined that the minimum speed required to escape the Earth's gravity is 6.83 miles (11.2 kilometres) per second. A scene from the movie From the Earth to the Moon, based on the work by Jules Verne. Jules Verne described the effects of weightlessness on space travellers.

The Father of Astronautics

The Russian K. E. Tsiolkowski was the first scientist to dedicate himself to the basic problems of space travel. One basic idea he proposed was the use of liquid fuels instead of solid ones.

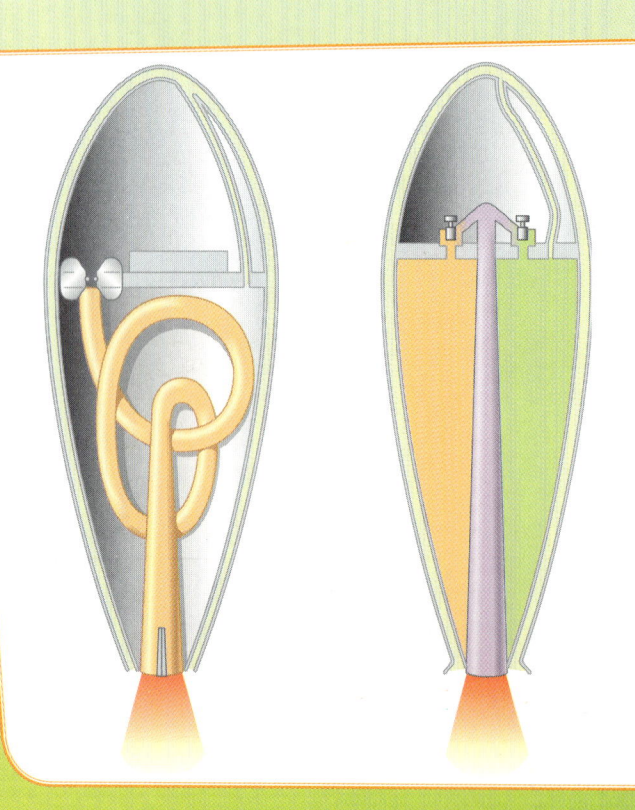

The first rocket prototypes created by Tsiolkowski in 1914 and 1915.

The liquid fuels proposed by Tsiolkowski included hydrogen, oxygen, and carbon hydroxide. The first rocket prototypes created by Tsiolkowski in 1914 and 1915.

Esnault-Pelterie
The Frenchman R. Esnault-Pelterie designed various propulsion motors and furthered the possibilities of using nuclear fuels.

Goddard
The American R. H. Goddard succeeded in launching a rocket using liquid oxygen and alcohol fuel, just as Tsiolkowski had proposed years before.

Von Braun
The German engineer Wernher von Braun constructed the famous V-2.

Oberth
Another German, Hermann Oberth collaborated on the production of the V-2 and after that he continued his studies on spaceship propulsion in the United States.

The deadly V-2 flying bombs were the precursors of present-day missiles; after the war they served as rockets at the start of the Space Race.

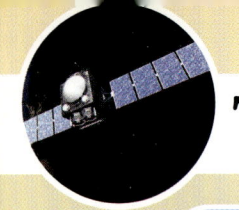

The Space Race

Once World War II was over, the old Allies, the United States and the Soviet Union and began special programs designed to reach the Moon. That became known as the Space Race.

How does a Rocket Work?

The first step in the Space Race involved building rockets that were capable of overcoming the Earth's gravity. Goddard had already succeeded in launching a rocket using liquid fuel, and the German V-2s had crossed the English Channel to bomb England. All these rockets, plus the ones that were developed subsequently, work the same way. A simple rocket consists of a propulsion chamber where the liquid fuel is burned, and that expels gases at more than 5,000 degrees Fahrenheit. For the purpose, the turbines have to be very durable so they don't melt. The escaping gases propel the rocket in the opposite direction. The payload is located at the opposite end; that may be other rockets or a space capsule.

The principle of the propulsion rocket. The oxidizing agent (1) makes it possible for the fuel to burn; the pump or gas impeller (2) pumps the fuel from the tank to the motor (3), where the fuel generates gas as it burns.

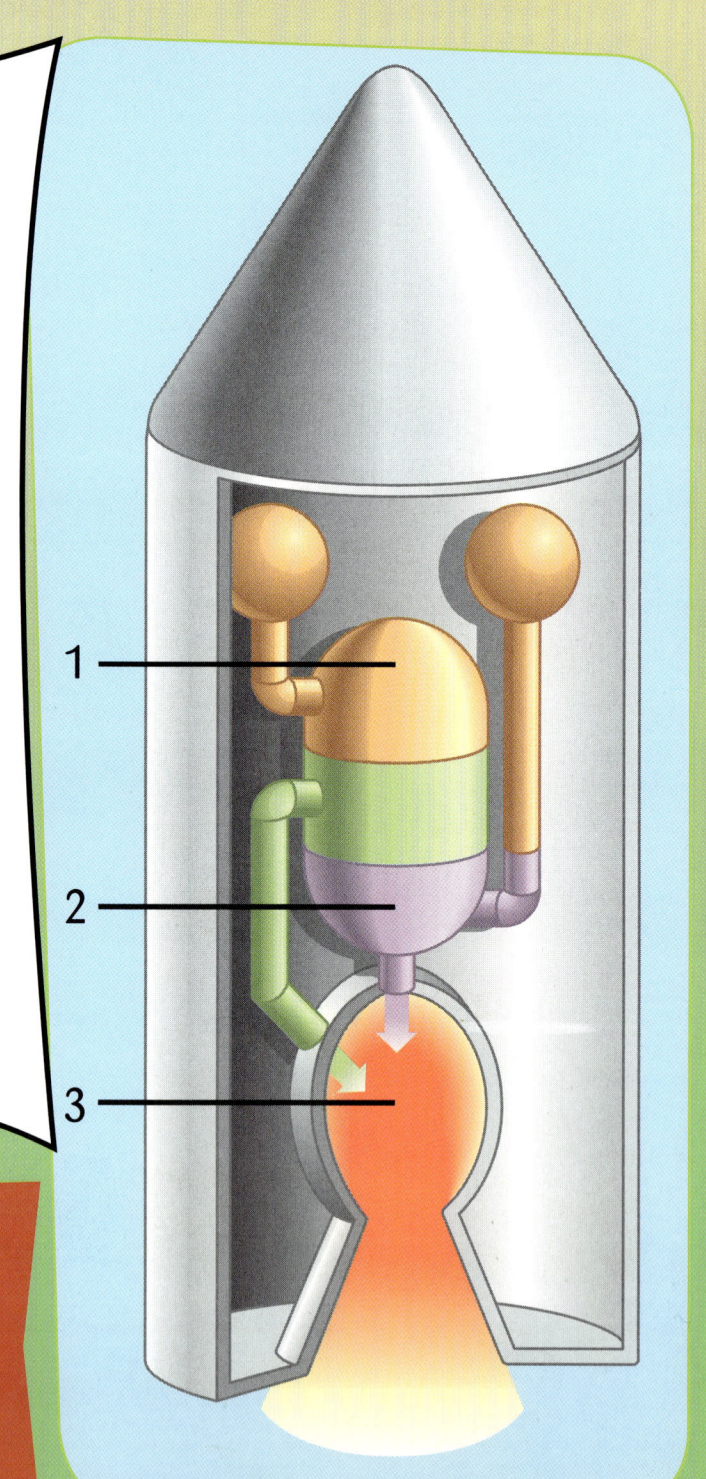

The Starting Gun

The Space Race officially began on July 29, 1955. On that day, the United States announced that it would construct and launch into space an artificial satellite that would enter into orbit around the Earth and take photographs of our planet. On August 1, 1955, three days after the American announcement, the Soviets also announced their intention to build and put into orbit a similar satellite.

The gigantic rocket Saturn 5 (110 m high and 2,700 metric tonnes in weight) made it possible for humans to reach the Moon.

How does a Rocket Work?

A simple rocket consists of a propulsion chamber where the liquid fuel is burned, and that expels gases at more than 5,000 degrees Fahrenheit. For that purpose, the turbines have to be very durable so they don't melt. The escaping gases propel the rocket in the opposite direction. The payload is located at the opposite end; that may be other rockets or a space capsule.

The First Artificial Satellite

On October 4, 1957, Soviet scientists put into orbit the first artificial satellite to orbit around the Earth; it was named Sputnik I. Space exploration had begun. That first satellite was small, no bigger than a large ball; it was silver in colour and had several antennae.

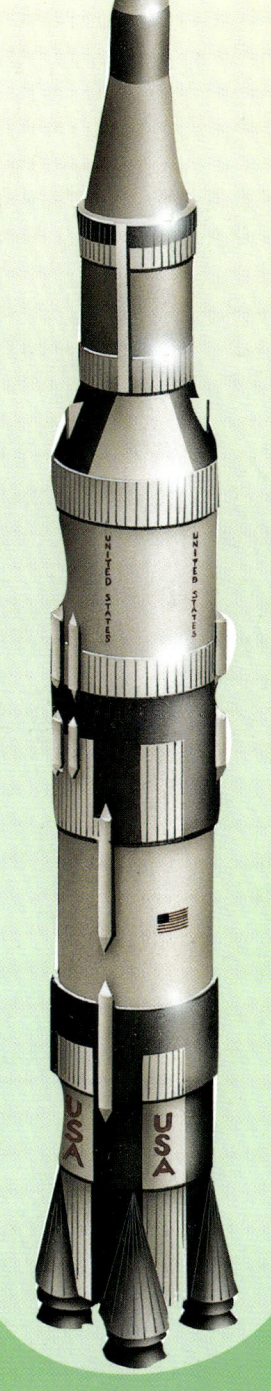

Four months after Sputnik I was launched (in the illustration) the first American satellite, Explorer I, was put into orbit.

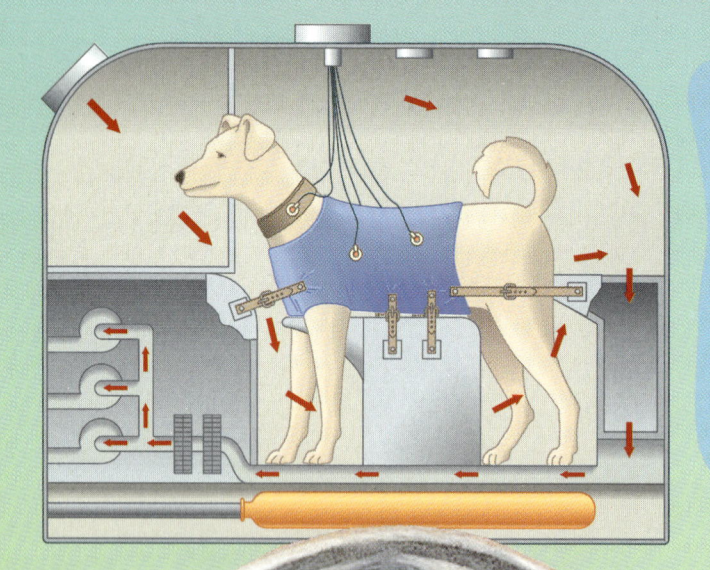

The First Living Creature in Space

On November 3, 1957, the Russians put a new satellite into orbit; it was named Sputnik II, and it carried inside it a Siberian Husky named Laika, who became the first living being to leave the Earth and venture into space.

Travelling Monkeys and Rats

While the Soviet scientists were using Siberian Huskies as astronauts, the Americans opted to use rats and monkeys. Flights involving monkeys were more successful; they provided valuable information for subsequent manned flights.

NASA (the National Aeronautics and Space Administration) was formed in July, 1958; it is the American civilian organization that deals with all matters involving aeronautics.

Men in Space

When construction techniques for rockets had reached a certain level that allowed launching a large capsule, and experiments with animals had demonstrated that it was possible to live in space, the two great national powers went a step farther, and for the first time humans succeeded in leaving the planet. A new age had begun.

Yuri Gagarin

The pilot Yuri Gagarin, became the first person to travel into space, on April 12, 1961. He did so on board a small capsule named Vostok 1. His flight lasted just a few hours, during which he made one revolution around the Earth.

John Glenn

John H. Glenn made a couple of trips around the Earth, and he remained in communication with ground control from his spaceship; these communications were broadcast to the public, and caused a major sensation.

The Mercury Project

Many other launches, both Soviet and American, followed the first two manned flights into space. The capsules were tight quarters that had room for only one crew member. The American flights involving a single crew member were designated the Mercury project.

A Mercury capsule after landing at sea.

The Apollo Mission

After the success of the first manned space flights, NASA began the Apollo project at the end of 1966, with the ambitious plan of putting a man on the Moon. Until that was achieved three years later, a number of increasingly complex tests were conducted by launching capsules containing two or three astronauts, having one of them leave the spacecraft for the first time, and sending satellites to the Moon to explore the terrain before making a manned landing. The last preparatory step involved a manned flight around our satellite.

An American space capsule landing in the ocean.

A Soviet space capsule landing in Siberia.

Victims of the Space Race

On January 27, 1967, before the launching of the first Apollo spaceship, an equipment failure in the rocket equipment caused a fire, and the three astronauts, Grissom, Chafee, and White, were burned to death. In mid-1967 the Soviet cosmonaut V. Komarov was killed when the parachute of the first Soyuz spaceship failed to open and the spacecraft crashed on its return to Earth. The worst disasters, however, occurred on January 28, 1986, when the seven astronauts of the Challenger died in an explosion during takeoff, and February 1, 2003, when the spacecraft Columbia disintegrated during reentry, killing the seven crew members.

Men in Space

When construction techniques for rockets had reached a certain level that allowed launching a large capsule, and experiments with animals had demonstrated that it was possible to live in space, the two great national powers went a step farther, and for the first time humans succeeded in leaving the planet. A new age had begun.

Yuri Gagarin

The pilot Yuri Gagarin, became the first person to travel into space, on April 12, 1961. He did so on board a small capsule named Vostok 1. His flight lasted just a few hours, during which he made one revolution around the Earth.

John Glenn

John H. Glenn made a couple of trips around the Earth, and he remained in communication with ground control from his spaceship; these communications were broadcast to the public, and caused a major sensation.

The Mercury Project

Many other launches, both Soviet and American, followed the first two manned flights into space. The capsules were tight quarters that had room for only one crew member. The American flights involving a single crew member were designated the Mercury project.

A Mercury capsule after landing at sea.

The Apollo Mission

After the success of the first manned space flights, NASA began the Apollo project at the end of 1966, with the ambitious plan of putting a man on the Moon. Until that was achieved three years later, a number of increasingly complex tests were conducted by launching capsules containing two or three astronauts, having one of them leave the spacecraft for the first time, and sending satellites to the Moon to explore the terrain before making a manned landing. The last preparatory step involved a manned flight around our satellite.

An American space capsule landing in the ocean.

A Soviet space capsule landing in Siberia.

Victims of the Space Race

On January 27, 1967, before the launching of the first Apollo spaceship, an equipment failure in the rocket equipment caused a fire, and the three astronauts, Grissom, Chafee, and White, were burned to death. In mid-1967 the Soviet cosmonaut V. Komarov was killed when the parachute of the first Soyuz spaceship failed to open and the spacecraft crashed on its return to Earth. The worst disasters, however, occurred on January 28, 1986, when the seven astronauts of the Challenger died in an explosion during takeoff, and February 1, 2003, when the spacecraft Columbia disintegrated during reentry, killing the seven crew members.

Preparing for the Great Voyage

In 1963, America instituted the Gemini Program, which consisted of launching manned space capsules containing two astronauts. Within a few months, the Soviets did the same. On July 31, 1964, the American space probe Ranger 7 crashed onto the surface of the Moon after taking four thousand close-up photographs. On March 18, 1965, the Soviet cosmonaut Leonov completed the first space walk connected to his spaceship by a cable. In December, 1965, two American spaceships, Gemini 6 and 7 docked together for the first time in space, thereby demonstrating the possibility of carrying out this type of operation. On February 3, 1966, the Soviet space probe Luna 9 landed gently on the surface of the Moon and began to transmit photographs. In June of the same year, the American probe Surveyor 1 also landed on the Moon.

Landing on the Moon

The Definitive Flight: On 16 July, 1969, Apollo 11 blasted off from Cape Kennedy en route to the Moon. Three days later it entered the orbit of the Moon.

Many had feared that the surface of the Moon was made of dust and that any spacecraft that landed would immediately sink. Experience showed otherwise.

On 20 July, 1969, Neil Armstrong and Edwin Aldrin descended to the surface of the Moon onboard the lunar module Eagle and made a soft landing.
In the early hours of 21 July, 1969, Armstrong opened the hatch, climbed down the ladder, and stepped on to the surface of the Moon, followed shortly by Aldrin.

Six times on the Moon

There have been six other manned expeditions to the Moon (Apollo 12 to Apollo 17) since the first landing.

Neil Armstrong said these famous words on television: "That's one small step for [a] man, one giant leap for mankind."

There have been six other manned expeditions to the Moon (Apollo 12 to Apollo 17) since the first landing.

A Historic Step

When Neil Armstrong climbed down the ladder of the lunar module and steeped onto the ground, the module's television cameras captured the moment and transmitted it to the Earth, where hundreds of millions of spectators were able to follow the event directly. The astronauts were moving around and were able to jump effortlessly due to the reduced gravitational force.

Space Exploration Beyond the Moon

In the 1960s, the conquest of the Moon was one of the most important programmes carried out by NASA and by Soviet scientists. But at the same time there were other projects of greater scope and duration that targeted longer-term results: space exploration beyond the Moon.

Conquering the Planets

Between the years 1962 and 1973 both space powers launched numerous satellites headed for the main planets of the Solar System; they obtained closer photographs and some data about their surface. In the subsequent years, it has finally been possible to use the photos in drawing up maps of those planets, and to touch down on some of them.

Life on Mars?: In 1970, the Russian spacecraft Venera 7 landed successfully on the surface of Venus, and other spaceships in this series repeated the feat in the following years. The American spacecraft Viking I and Viking II arrived on Mars in 1976 and carried out experiments to search for signs of life, but they found none.

And Beyond...: Voyager I and II were launched in 1977. They passed close to Jupiter in 1979; Saturn in 1980 and 1981; Uranus in 1986; and Neptune in 1989.

In 1997, Mars Pathfinder deposited a vehicle onto the surface of Mars.

Probing Venus: In 1978, Pioneer Venus 2 launched several probes on parachutes onto the surface of Venus.

International Cooperation

The Space Race was an extremely costly project, and international financial problems caused both the Russians and the Americans to suspend some of their programs. That opened the door for cooperation with other countries, including the European countries that belonged to the ESA (European Space Agency). Ever since the end of the 1970s, various joint space probes and scientific satellites have succeeded in expanding our knowledge of the solar system, with results that are sometimes spectacular.

On March 14, 1986, the European space probe Giotto met up with Halley's Comet and succeeded in photographing it and analyzing it up close.

Skylab, the first American space station was put into orbit in 1973; as a result it became possible for teams of astronauts to stay in space for several months.

On November 28, 1983, the American transport Columbia put the European Spacelab into orbit.

Space Laboratories and Stations

Since outer space has no atmospheric layer like the one that covers the Earth, it offers many advantages for astronomical observations. As a result, several laboratories have been constructed and placed into stationary orbit around our planet. The smallest of them are operated from ground control, but the most elaborate ones have been incorporated into space stations; in other words, permanent laboratories occupied by astronauts who stay in them for several months as they carry on their work. Space launches such as Discovery perform regular flights between these stations and the Earth, transporting materials and astronauts. The goal is to construct a large space station where the astronauts can carry on their work under favourable conditions, and that will serve as an intermediate step for more distant expeditions.

An International Space Station

Construction work on the ISS (International Space Station) began in 1998; it involves cooperation among Americans, Russians, and Europeans. At the start of 2001 parts of the ISS space station were ready for habitation.

The ISS, the first step in colonizing space.

The first Russian space station was Salyut, which was put into orbit shortly after the American station. The Russian space station Mir began work in the 1980s as a substitute for Salyut, and it remained in use nearly until 2000. On June 29, 1995, the American space launch Atlantis and the Russian space station Mir successfully docked at an altitude of 244 miles (400 kilometres) and a speed of over 17,000 miles (28,000 kilometres)/hour; then the astronauts passed from one spacecraft to the other.

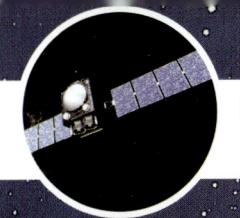

The Future of Astronautics

Scarcely a dozen years passed from the launching of the first man-made satellite—a simple metal sphere that sent out a beep—to the landing of men on the Moon, and from that time onward space has been filled with satellites, spaceships, and space stations. Proposals even include colonizing the Moon and establishing bases on nearby planets such as Mars.

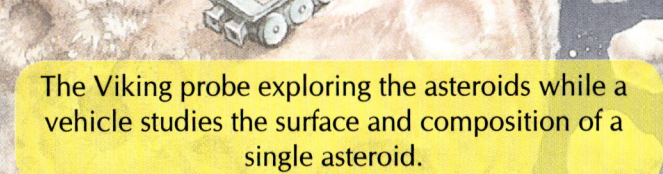

The Viking probe exploring the asteroids while a vehicle studies the surface and composition of a single asteroid.

Projects Underway

In the past two decades aeronautics has been characterised chiefly by international cooperation, which has intensified since the collapse of the Soviet Union. The United States (NASA), Russia, Europe (ESA), and Japan (NASDA) are working together on projects that require great economic investments and careful scientific and technical research from hundreds of teams spread around the globe.

At the end of 2001 a geological map of the surface of Mars was completed with the help of Mars Surveyor, and in 2003 several probes will land on the red planet in order to gather more samples of the soil and continue studies for installing a possible base.

The Cluster II mission of NASA and ESA began in July and August of 2000. This involves four satellites travelling in formation to measure the solar magnetic fields and storms.

So Near, Yet So Far

While ESA's Integral Astronomical Satellite, which was launched at the end of 2001, records emissions of cosmic rays to verify the origin of the universe, many of the satellites launched throughout 2001 are intended to study Earth: the ozone layer, weather forecasting, studies of glaciers, measuring vegetation, climatic changes, and so forth.

A Space Tourist

In April, 2001, an American multimillionaire, Dennis Tito, became the first space tourist.

The new instruments for exploring and studying space that are now available guarantee that many of the mysteries of the universe will be revealed in the present decade.

A study of Saturn's rings is planned for 2004; a probe will be sent to its satellite Titan, where it will land on the surface. The surface of Mars contains lots of metallic oxides, which give it the red colour; they may be a source of oxygen.

Round Trip

It is planned that a space probe launched in 2002 will land on the asteroid Nereus, gather samples of the soil, and return to Earth in 2008.

A Base on the Moon

The desire to colonize other heavenly bodies will probably begin with the Moon. The exploration of its surface carried out by the astronauts, the numerous analyses and studies conducted by robots and stationary satellites since that time, and instruments placed on its surface will help make that project a reality. The second planet to be colonized will probably be Mars, which offers similar conditions for constructing bases.

Vestiges of ice were discovered on the surface of the Moon in 1999, so it may contain some water in frozen form.

Space stations around the Earth will be the first step in interplanetary travel; they will probably use the Moon as a launching site, as shown in the illustration.

Astronauts

Space exploration is a highly technical activity, the success of which depends heavily on robots and computers. Still, the human presence is required for many activities. Astronauts are the ones to carry out those tasks, and for that they need very special training.

The Space Helmet

The space helmet has a face shield that protects the astronaut against both the intense visible light given off by the Sun and dangerous cosmic radiation.

Space Suits

Space suits have evolved a lot over the years. Special fabrics have been devised, and the helmets have been improved to provide the proper environment for the person who has to work inside the suit. These suits are designed for performing tasks in space outside the spaceship and for moving about the surface of celestial bodies. The first astronauts were attached to their spaceship by cables. Now they have devices that they can control for moving freely around them; but for safety reasons, the cables are still used.

It is necessary to maintain a pressure of around 30 pounds (13.6 kg) per square inch (1013 hPa) inside both the spaceship and the space suit. The oxygen supply devices of independent space suits make it possible for an astronaut to remain outside the spacecraft for several hours.

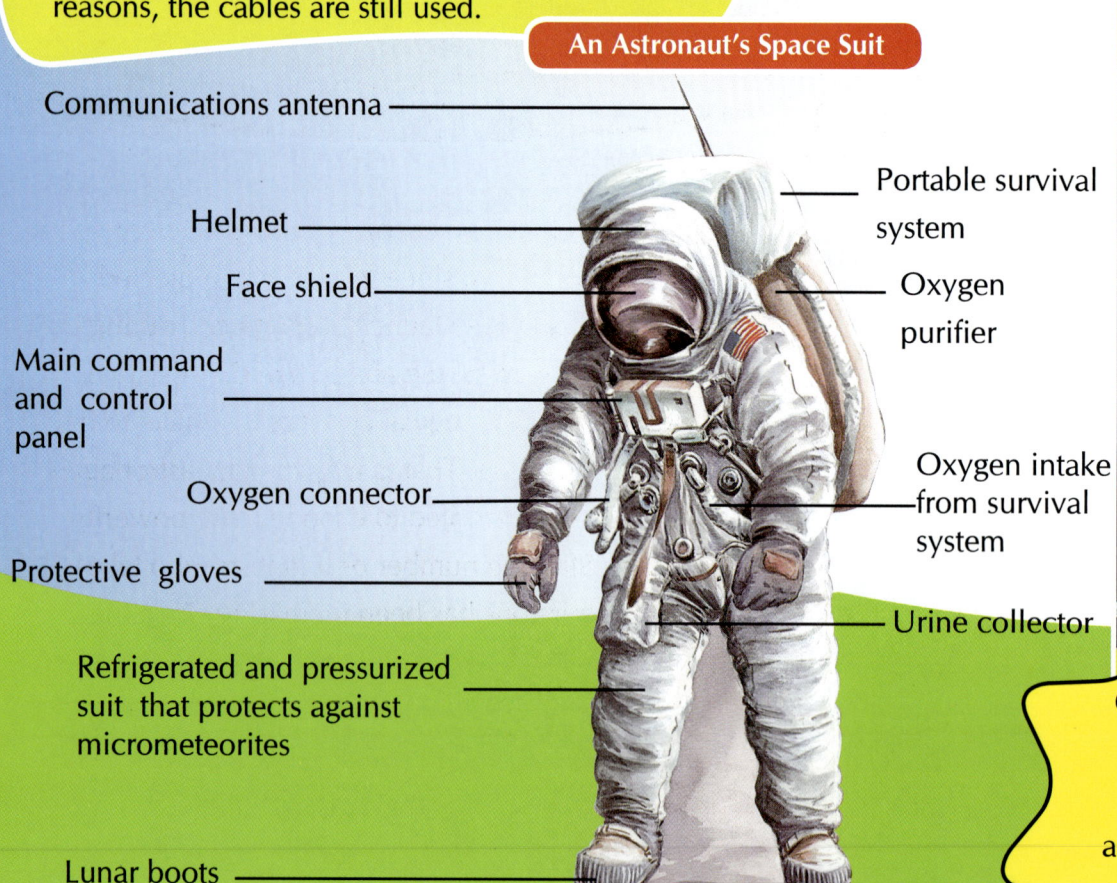

An Astronaut's Space Suit

- Communications antenna
- Helmet
- Face shield
- Main command and control panel
- Oxygen connector
- Protective gloves
- Refrigerated and pressurized suit that protects against micrometeorites
- Lunar boots
- Portable survival system
- Oxygen purifier
- Oxygen intake from survival system
- Urine collector

Communication devices are essential for astronauts outside their spacecraft.

174

Life in a Spaceship

The first space flights lasted just a few hours, but as they grew longer it became necessary to provide more complex equipment to assure that conditions remained acceptable for the astronauts. In the first space stations, such as the Russian Mir, the astronauts didn't have much space for moving around freely, and they had to do all their activities in an all-purpose compartment. However, the new space stations such as the International Space Station (ISS) currently under construction are complex installations that are comparable to the ones that exist on Earth in areas of extreme conditions, such as Antarctica. The ISS consists of several modules where the astronauts work, sleep, and have adequate room for rest breaks.

During the launch of a spaceship, the human body weighs up to ten times more than normal. Weightlessness, the absence of gravity, causes decalcification of the bones after an extended period of time. During a space mission, each astronaut is responsible for several specific tasks. The greatest difficulty they have seems to be living together for several days in such a restricted area.

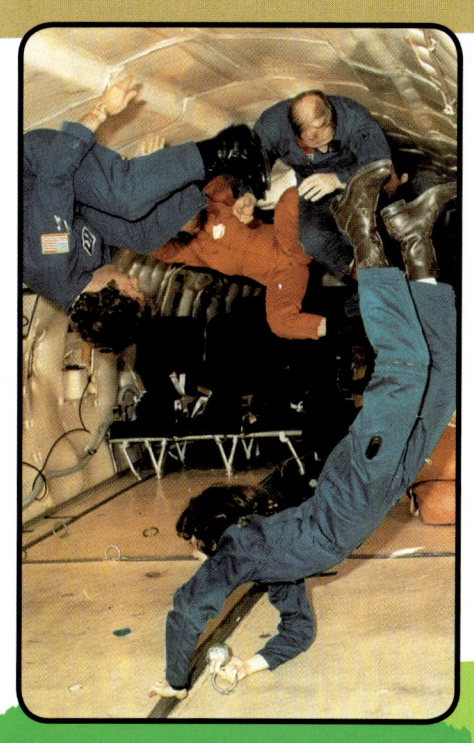

Inside a training room for astronauts; here they are getting used to weightlessness.

Difficult Training

In order to travel into space, one has to be in very fine physical condition, since the body is subjected to great stress during the launch. In addition, during extended stays in space, the absence of Earth's gravity produces major physiological changes that have to be offset by good training. That is why the first astronauts were test pilots accustomed to experiencing powerful acceleration. Still, the number of scientists who take part in space missions has been increasing since the 1990s. Although they have to be in perfect health, the new technology facilitates their adaptation to space. Future travellers who go to the Moon and Mars as tourists will have to be healthy, but the spacecraft will compensate for many of the present inconveniences by creating artificial gravity, among other things.

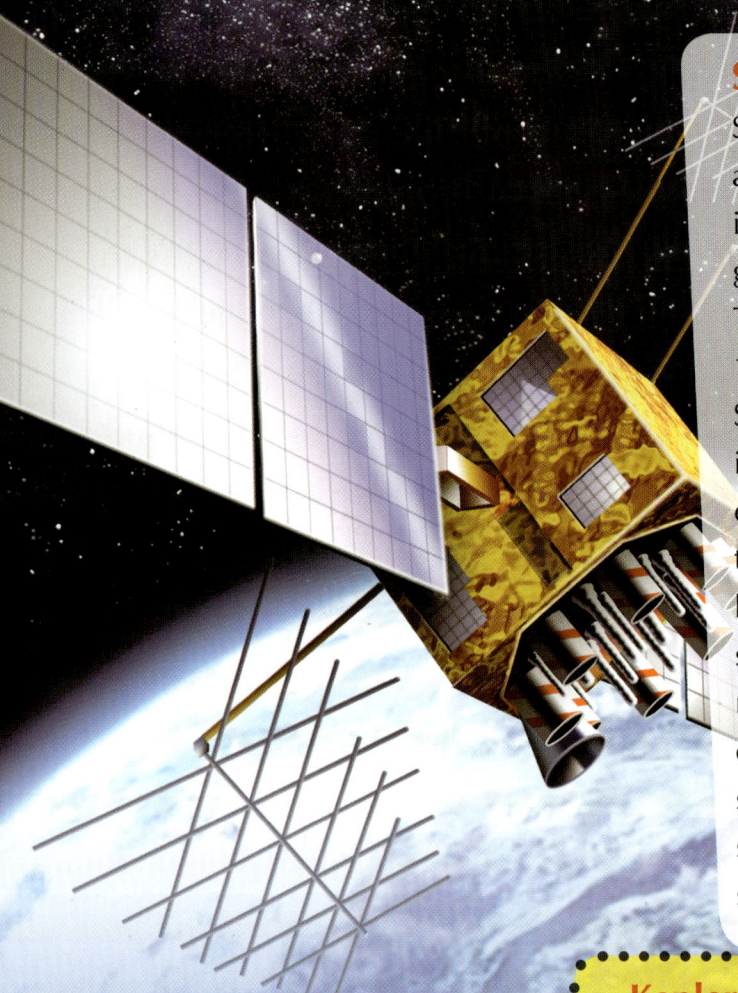

Satellites all the way!!!

Satellites are key to carry a space mission. Over a thousand of satellites have been blasted off into the space. While some endeavour brought glory, others have failed to arrest desired result. The world's first artificial satellite, the Sputnik 1, was launched by the Soviet Union in 1957. Sometimes these satellites have crashed back into the atmosphere. Other fortunate ones have escaped the Earth's orbit and are flying off into the Solar System. These man-made satellites are hovering around the space. Each satellite is on a special task which varies as per the need of the research. The satellites fall under these following categories-military and civilian observation satellites, communication satellites, navigation satellites, weather satellites, and research satellites.

Application of high-end technology and leveraging to reveal the hidden mysteries of the Universe, NASA has ventured into myriad observation, some of their latest ventures include- Dawn, Kepler and the Juno.

Kepler

Christened in the honour of the 17th –century German astronomer Johannes Kepler, Kepler is a space observatory launched in March 2009 by NASA to discover Earth-like planets orbiting other stars. Kepler's only instrument is a photometer that continually monitors the brightness of over 1,45,000 main sequence stars in a fixed field of view. Kepler is a relatively low-cost project, focused on science missions.

Dawn

A million dollar experiment, the robotic spacecraft was launched on September 27, 2007. Dawn is on a mission to collect data's on Vesta and Ceres, the two largest members of the asteroid belt. Dawn was the first spacecraft to visit Vesta, and is scheduled to be the first to visit Ceres. If it successfully reaches Ceres, it will also be the first spacecraft to orbit two separate extraterrestrial bodies, using ion thrusters to travel between its targets.

Juno

This extravagant spacecraft will help us to understand the planet Jupiter in a better way. Juno is a NASA New Frontiers mission to the planet Jupiter. It was launched from Cape Canaveral Air Force Station on August 5, 2011. The spacecraft is to be placed in a polar orbit to study the planet's composition, gravity field, magnetic field, and polar magnetosphere. Juno shall take us to the history behind the formation of the planet Jupiter, and also other questions such as whether the planet has a rocky core, the amount of water present within the deep atmosphere, and how the planet's mass is distributed is expected to be answered. Juno requires a five-year cruise to Jupiter, arriving around July 4, 2016. The spacecraft will orbit Jupiter 33 times during one Earth year. Once Juno enters into its orbit, infrared and microwave instruments will begin to measure the thermal radiation emanating from deep within Jupiter's atmosphere. The Juno mission is set to conclude in October 2017, after completing 33 orbits around Jupiter, when the probe will be de-orbited to crash into Jupiter.

Interesting Facts About Neil Armstrong

- Neil Armstrong was a super active kid; he has earned the Eagle Scout badge in Boy Scouts.
- More than Six hundred million eyes were glued to the Television who silently accompanied Armstrong in his journey.
- He was awarded the Presidential Medal of Freedom, which is the highest civilian honour of the US government.
- He stopped signing autographs after he found out that people were selling them on the internet.

Silver Foot

Fantasies in our forebear's tales were realised by one man- on the epic date of July 21, 1969. Neil. A. Armstrong became the first man to create history when his spacecraft Apollo 1, landed on the moon. He along with his companion Buzz Aldrin set their foot on the Moon and meandered around. Armstrong's famous words upon being the first man on the Moon were **"That's one small step for man, one giant leap for mankind**" Did you know? Mr. Armstrong was an experienced pilot and had fought in the Korean War where he flew magnificent fighters from aircraft carriers. He flew over 200 different types of aircraft during his career. Neil Armstrong set out for his final abode on August 25, 2012. The world will miss the hero who not only conquered hearts of millions, but his feats stretches to the Moon.

If you desire to see yourself in the same footing to that of Neil Armstrong, you first need to prepare scrupulously to make it to the space. Here are some tips which might prove useful.

- Get into fervent flying lessons. Unless you have devoted a minimum of 1000 hours flying a jet aircraft; you are not eligible to be an astronaut.
- Take special care of your diet; you have to be strong enough to carry a space suit which weighs approximately 280 pounds—without the astronaut—and it takes 45 minutes to enrobe.
- Get ready to give up on your favorite food as an astronaut is allotted 3.8 pounds of food per day. Edibles are individually packaged and stored for ease of handling in zero gravity. Foods are precooked or processed, so as to require no refrigeration, and are either ready to eat or can be simply prepared by adding water or by heating. With a sound mind and healthy body you shall touch the sky.
- You can carry a few vegetables along, but it must be consumed as early as possible before it gets rotten. Available condiments include salt, pepper, taco sauce, hot pepper, sauce, ketchup, mayonnaise, and mustard.
- Always be ready to take up challenges. Remember, hard work is the key to success. Only your sincerity and dedication towards the same will enable you to reach your goal.

The Big Bang Theory

We know that the Universe is expanding all the time. The galaxies are moving away from one another at different speeds according to the distance they are apart. The average speed of this movement is 20 kilometres per second for each million light-years of distance between galaxies. This is called **Hubble's constant.**

A Massive Fireball

What was the Universe like a long time ago? Most astronomers think that the galaxies must have been closer together than they are now. If we go further back in time to about 1,5000 million years ago, we can imagine an instant when all the galaxies and all the matter between them were closely packed together in a massive fireball. So we can work out from this that the Universe began at a certain point in the past.

Explosion

The Universe was a very dense place at its beginning, and it was in a state of violent expansion. This growth led to an explosion. In the scattering, some pieces clustered together into galaxies that are still travelling further and further apart. This is the state of the Universe as we know it today.

Hot and compressed: This theory which states that the Universe began in an enormous explosion is called the **Big Bang theory**. It states that around 15,000 million years ago at its very beginning, the Universe was extremely hot and compressed, and was expanding violently.

Cooling Down

By now the Universe has cooled a great deal, and the speed of expansion has decreased. Scientists are able to measure this by the red shift of the galaxies.

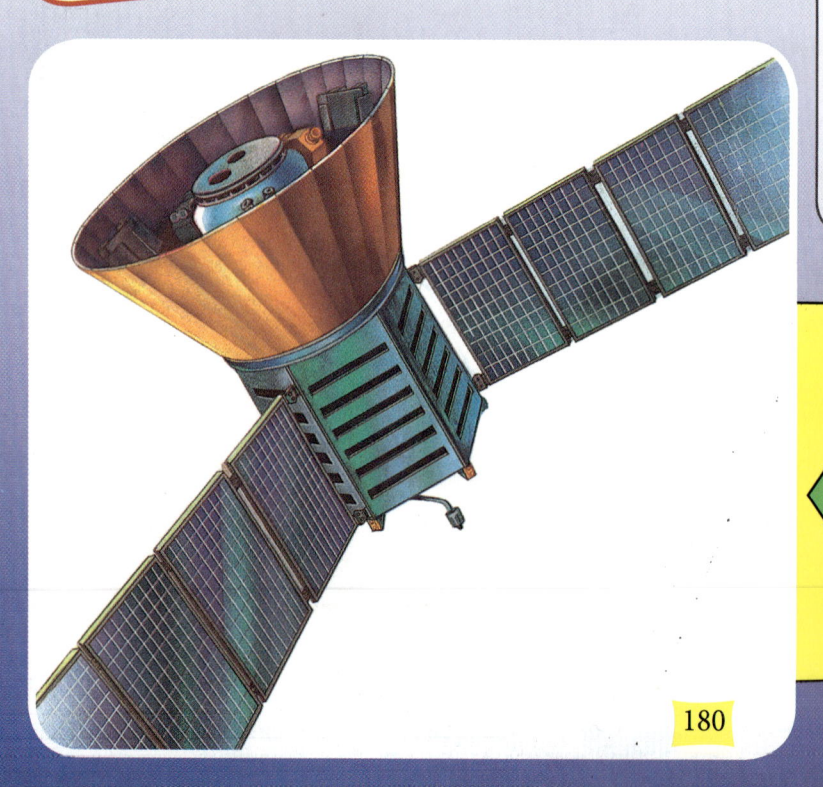

The COBE satellite has measured the heat of the first great explosion. This energy reaches us from all directions of outer space.

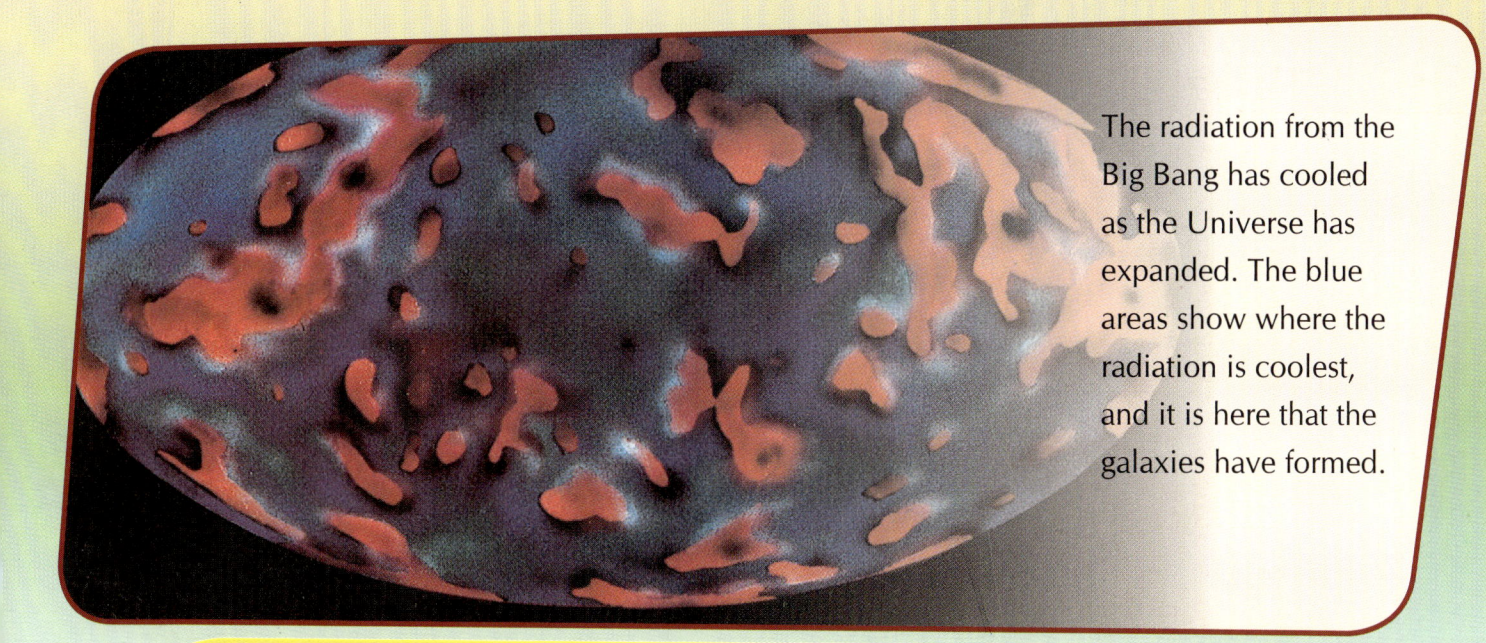

The radiation from the Big Bang has cooled as the Universe has expanded. The blue areas show where the radiation is coolest, and it is here that the galaxies have formed.

The Universe began around 15,000 million years ago in a powerful explosion [1] known as the Big Bang. In its first moments, the Universe expanded quickly [2], and it also cooled quickly. The radiation that filled the Universe at that time is what we can now measure as a weak background radiation. When the galaxies formed [3], the Universe began to look something like it does today [4], with galaxies moving away from each other at moderate speeds.

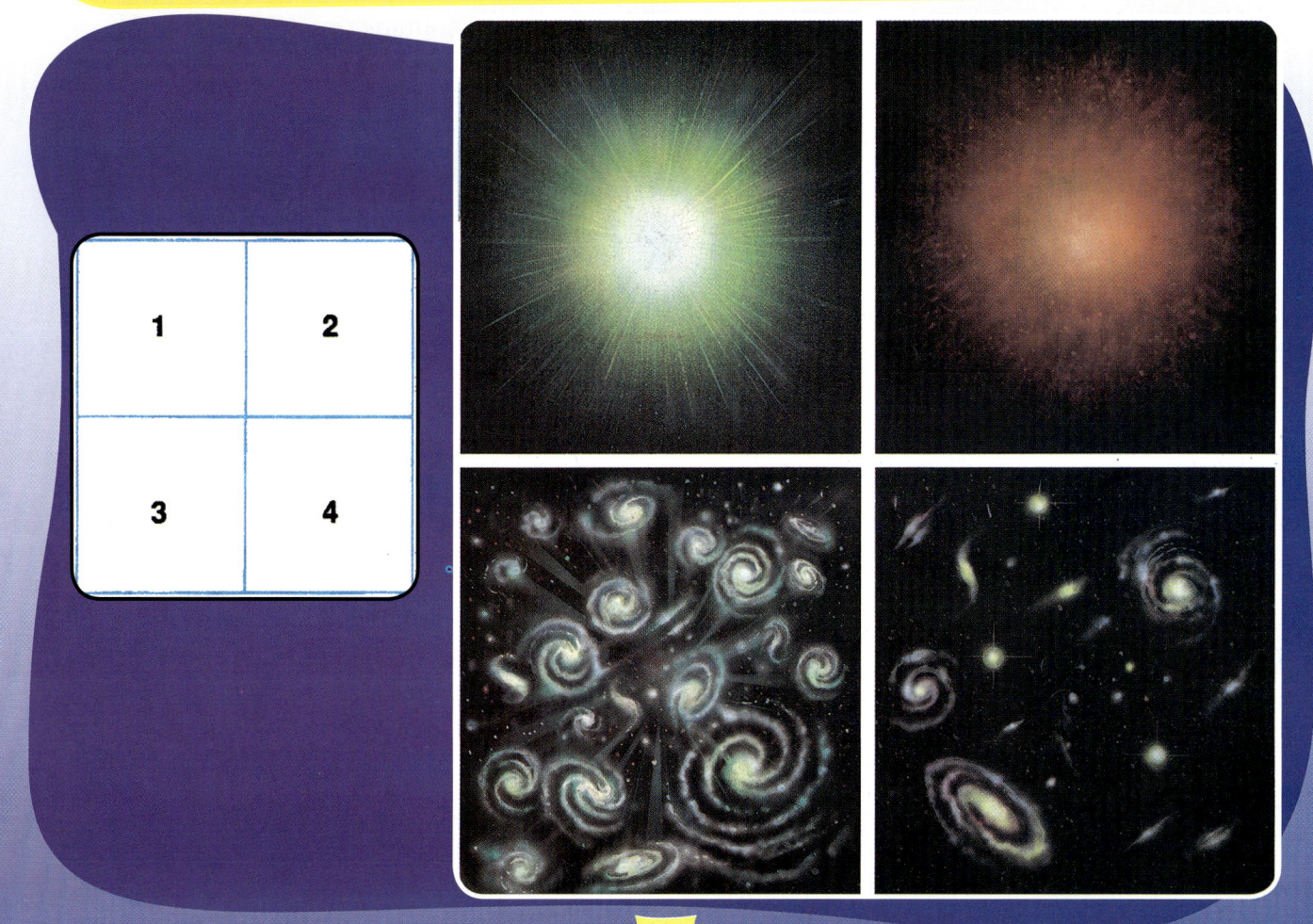

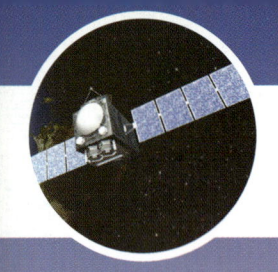

The incredible energy of the quasars

The further away from us an object is, the longer it takes for its light to reach us. So at the same time as we explore more deeply into space, we also look back in time. A galaxy which is, for example, 1,000 million light years away, is seen as it was 1,000 million years ago, the amount of time it has taken for its light to reach us. In this way, the most distant galaxies give us an opportunity to see what the Universe was like in the past.

Distant Galaxies

Young galaxies are the ones that formed shortly after the Universe began. But what are they like? Are they very different from the middle-aged galaxies, such as the Milky Way or our closest neighbours? To answer these questions we need to look at the most distant galaxies we know.

Quasars

In 1963, it was discovered that objects called **quasars** were receding from us at speeds of about one third the speed of light. According to Hubble's law, an object which recedes from us at this speed must be about 5000 million light years away, much further than any other galaxy known at that time. Today, scientists have discovered many quasars which are even further away, close to the furthest part of the Universe that we can see. Quasars are young galaxies that developed shortly after the Universe formed. They have a more brilliant nucleus than normal galaxies.

The radiation given out by a quasar can vary a lot over several months.

In the nucleus of a quasar, there is a very dense object which may be a **black hole**. This is an area with a strong gravitational pull that draws matter from the galaxy into it. Streams of high-energy electrons shoot out of the nucleus.

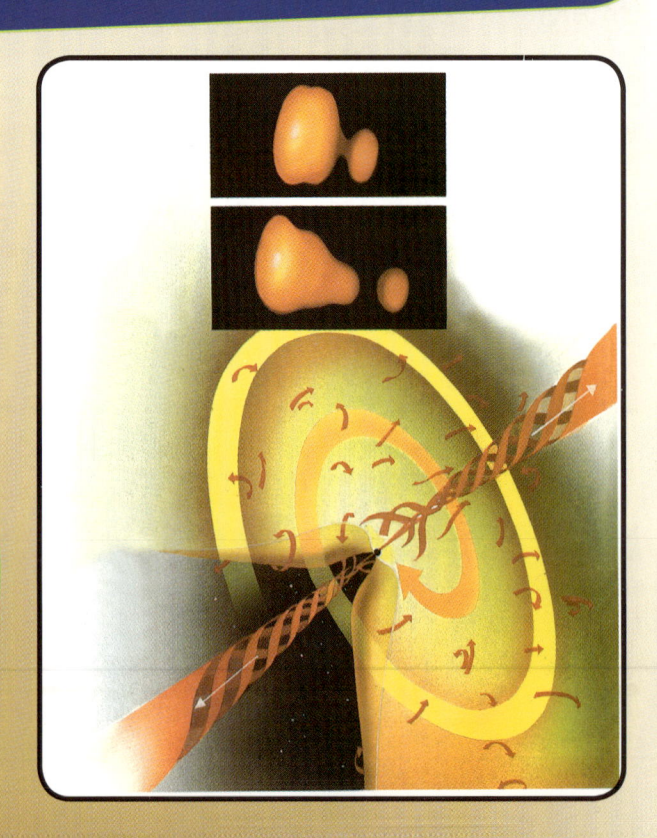

Quasars have a very bright nucleus [1] which is what makes it possible for us to see them despite their great distance. Within the bright nucleus, changes take place that are still not completely understood. These changes give off huge amounts of energy [2]. This energy escapes into space in the form of light and radio waves of radiation [3]. This is why many quasars are very intense sources of radio emissions.

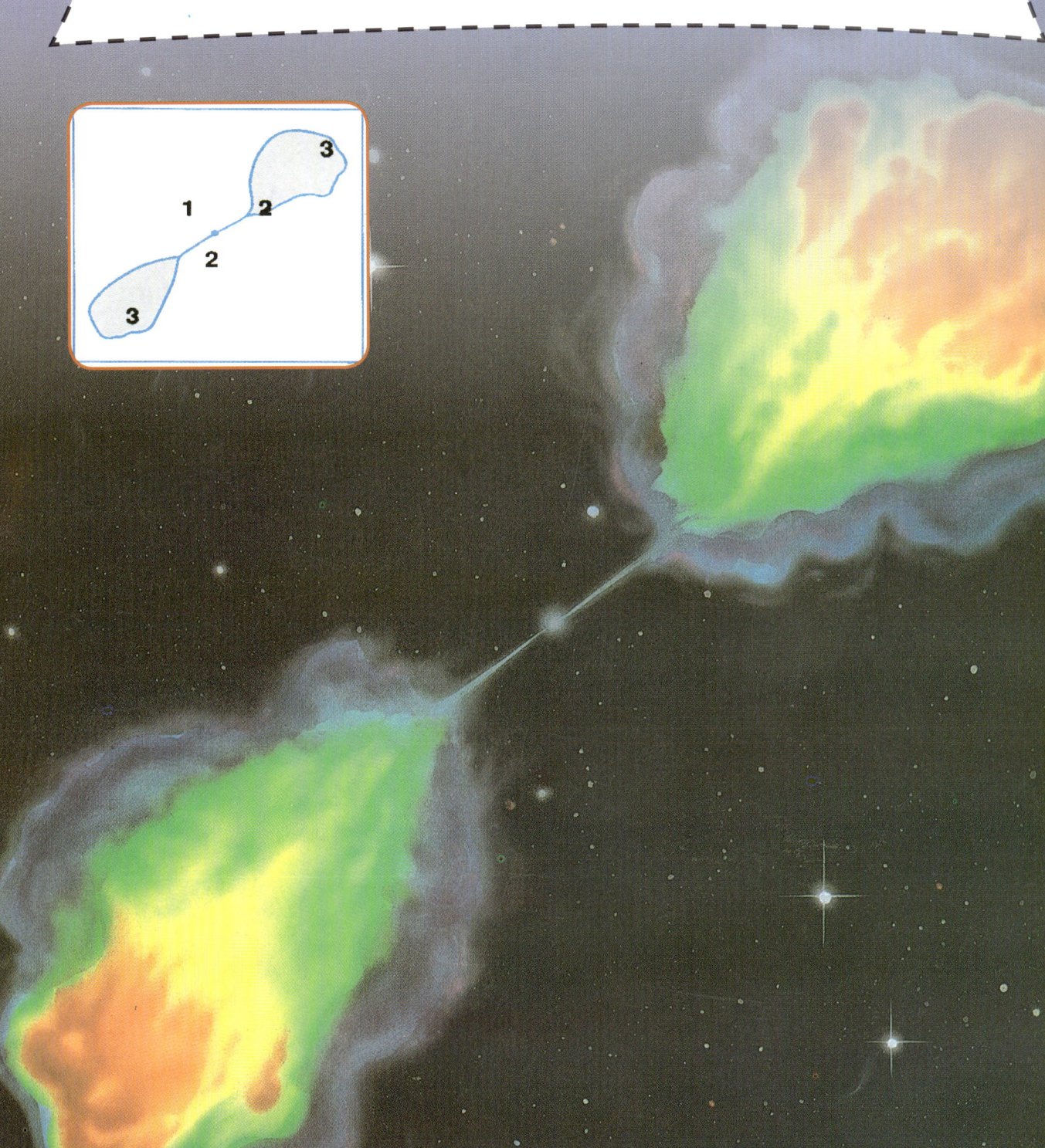

The Future of the Universe

During the first moments of the Big Bang, the Universe expanded at a great speed. Now the rate of this expansion has slowed down. But what is causing the Universe to slow down its growth?

Gravity

The force responsible for this slowing down is the gravitational pull among the galaxies. It was much greater when the Universe had just begun, when the galaxies were much closer together. Now that the galaxies are further apart, the force of attraction is much weaker, but the gravitational pull throughout time has managed to slow the expansion. Why are we interested in the slowing down of this expansion? This is because the future of the Universe depends on it. Scientists think two things can happen.

An Open Universe

It is possible that the expansion of the Universe, although it is slowing down, will never stop completely. The Universe will change very little over millions of years. Later, it will gradually become weaker and colder as all the galaxies die and no new stars are formed. This is called an open Universe.

An Closed Universe

It is also possible that the expansion is slowing down enough to bring it to a complete stop. The movement will reverse, as gravitational force pulls the galaxies together again. The Universe will contract, faster and faster, until it ends in a great final implosion. This is a closed Universe.

The future of the Universe depends on the strength of the gravitational pull. So if enough matter exists in the Universe, it will have enough gravitational pull to stop the growth of the Universe. But many cosmologists believe the expansion of the universe will never stop [1]. For the Universe to contract in the future [2], it would need ten times more matter than the amount it is currently known to contain. It is possible that a large amount of undiscovered dark matter exists in the Universe.

1

2

Even if the future of the Universe is not known with certainty, the future of Earth as a planet is completely determined by the Sun. Within 5,000 million years, the Sun will have burnt up all the hydrogen in its nucleus and will begin to swell until it turns into a red giant [1]. Seen from the Earth, the Sun will fill a large part of the sky. Its heat will evaporate the Earth's oceans and make the terrestrial atmosphere disappear [2]. This will be the end of Earth as a habitable planet.

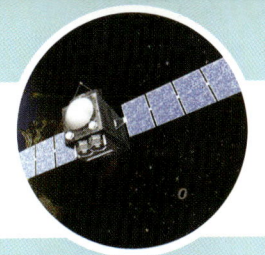

Activity: The Most Distant Visible Objects

When you look at the night sky, have you ever wondered what is the most distant object that you are able to see? You will almost certainly think that one of the stars you are looking at could be the most distant.

Distant Stars

The brightest stars, for example, are between 5 and 100 light years away. Most other stars visible to the naked eye are not more than a few thousand light-years away. But you can see stars that are a lot further away than this. These belong to the luminous band of the **Milky Way**. A typical distance to one of these stars could be over 10,000 light-years. Further away, the stars are partly blocked out by the dust of the galactic disc. So far, we have spoken only of the stars in our galaxy. Is there a more distant object, outside the Milky Way, that can be easily seen?

If you live in the northern hemisphere, it is more difficult to see an object from outside our galaxy with the naked eye. You can see the Andromeda galaxy (in the constellation of Andromeda) with the naked eye but it is easier to see it with binoculars when the sky is clear and the night dark. This galaxy is truly distant. It lies two million light years away from us.

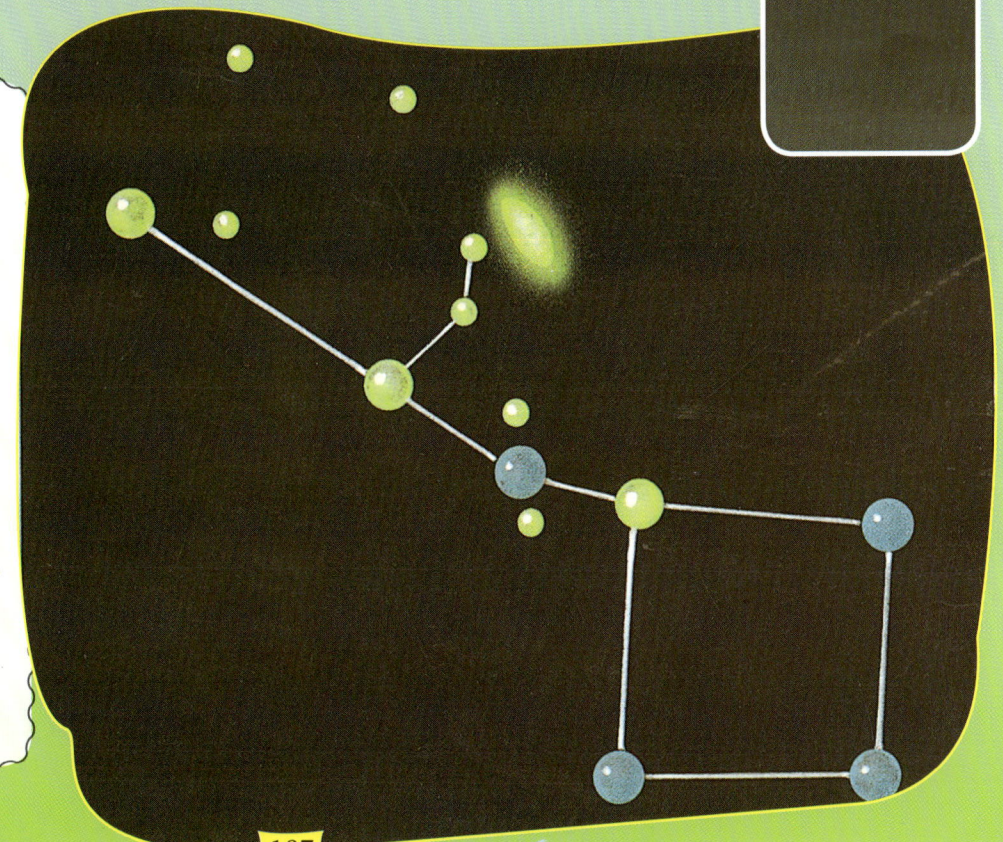

The Magellanic Clouds

In the southern skies, two small galaxies, called the Magellanic Clouds, can be seen easily with the naked eye. Both of them are fairly close to the celestial south pole. The Great Magellanic Cloud is found between the constellations of Dorado and Hydra. It is over 16,0000 light years away and is irregularly shaped. It may, in fact, be a barred spiral. The Small Magellanic Cloud is also irregular in shape and is 190,000 light years away.

Distances to Some Celestial Objects

Radius of the Earth	0.02 light-seconds
Distance to the Moon	1.3 light-seconds
Distance to the Sun	8 light-minutes
Distance to Pluto	5.5 light-hours
Distance to the closest star	4.3 light-years
Radius of the Milky Way	50,000 light-years
Closest galaxies	60,000 light-years
Andromeda galaxy	2 million light-years

Juvenile Steps

If you seek to pursue a career in astronomy, then mere inclination and interest towards the same won't serve your purpose. To map the stars and touch the sky one requires adopting the internal principles of the subject that would lead you to the goal. For this, you have to start from the nitty-gritty facts which are the key elements at the beginning of a race.

To study astronomy, the overall phenomena of the universe- how it functions, how everything relates, and where we fit in it needs to be very clear in our mind. We know that the universe is a gargantuan topic and the most difficult part arises when we think of its size scales, and other relative theories that are foreign to our knowledge. In a big universe, this can be a challenge. To your expediency the professional world is flooded with materials steering you in reaching the desired destination. But, before getting into curriculums, why not have some fun on our own.

For those challengers, when your mind and body is ready to explore the fancy world, you break yourself from the mundane surrounding and set out for the land of wonders. Stepping out from the confines of your city, you enter into the larger universe. With each step we will consider something a thousand times larger than the last. Observe the existing around you and contemplate how is all began, who was behind it and seek out an answer for yourself. Note down the thrilling specifics and try to capture the moments in your camera. These details hold hidden facts that might facilitate in your endeavour.

Begin from your very own land. Sail through the cities from one end to another, talk to the people around and try to get their philosophies of the world in which they live in. You will be surprised with the myriad imaginations and assumptions that you have amassed. As promised, the next step out will be an extravagant experience. By now you would have taken a 360 degree circle around the world. In a way, this assignment will give you a better picture from where to begin. It is indispensable to have a booming idea of the earth before setting out to the other world. Our dear planet if full of rich treasure that needs to be explored to satisfy our quench of knowledge and idea. Very importantly, you need to carry your own equipments along. Remember, an astronomer is an eloquent observer who is never gives up on details.

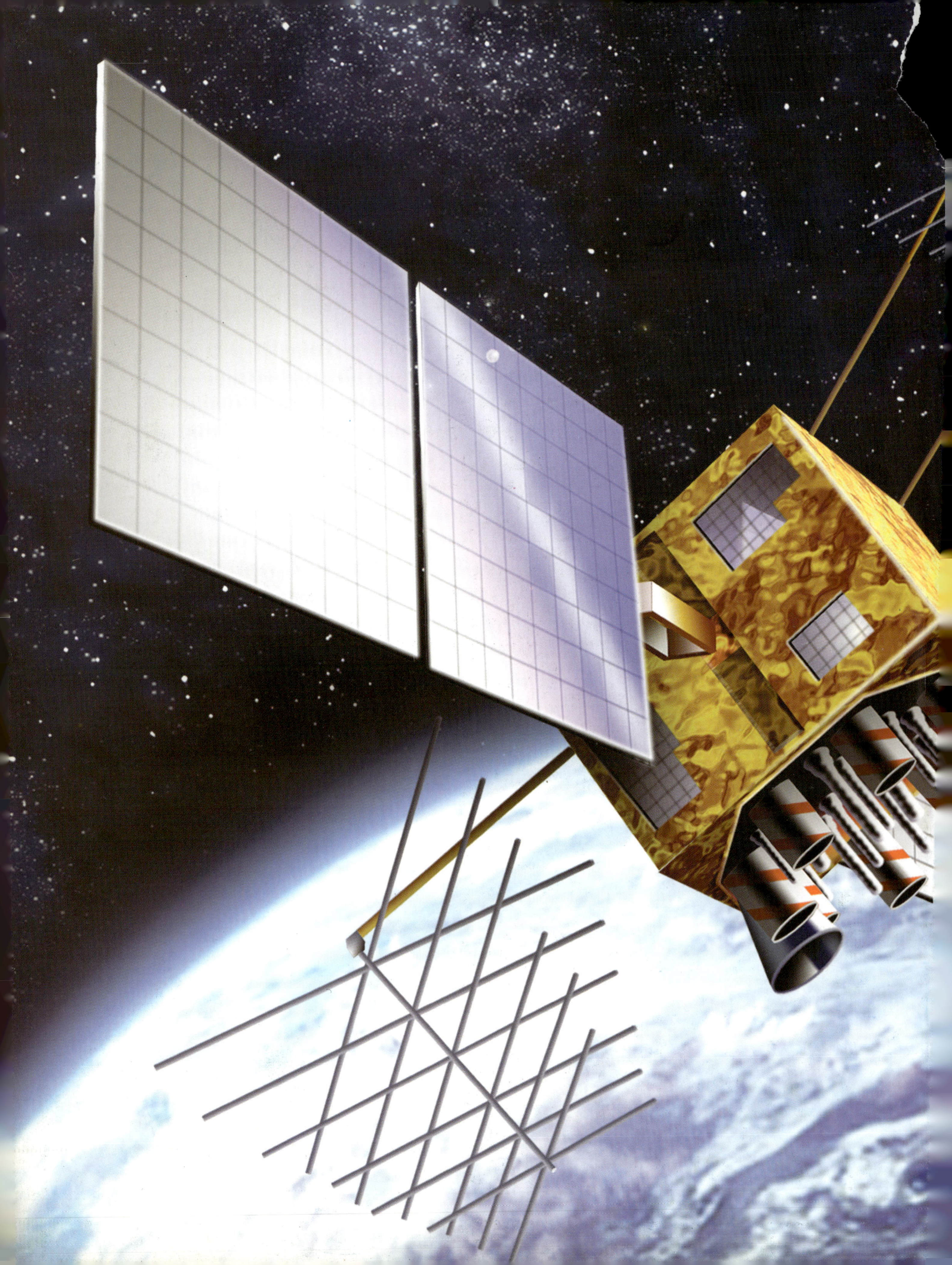